MEAL PREP & MEATLESS POWER COOKBOOK FOR VEGAN ATHLETES

200 High Protein Recipes to be Muscular and Plant-Based Diet Meal Plans for Beginners (2 in 1 Collection)

Joseph P. Turner

Copyright © 2019 by Joseph P. Turner All Rights Reserved.

No part of this publication may be reproduced, distributed, or transmitted in any form or by any means, including photocopying, recording, or other electronic or mechanical methods, or by any information storage and retrieval system without the prior written permission of the publisher, except in the case of very brief quotations embodied in critical reviews and certain other noncommercial uses permitted by copyright law.

DISCLAIMER

The information provided in this program is for educational purposes only. The author is not a doctor and this information shouldn't be taken as medical advice. You should get a physician's approval before attempting any of the information in this program. This program is designed for healthy adults of 18 years and older. If you have any existing injuries, conditions or health issues, please seek your physician's approval before attempting any type of information in this program. The author is not liable or responsible for any damages, resulting from the use of this program. The user acknowledges any risk of injury, caused or alleged, with the use of this information. If your physician advises to not use the information provided in the program, please abide by those orders.

Always seek the advice of your physician or another qualified health provider with any questions you may have regarding a medical condition. Never disregard professional medical advice or delay seeking it because of something you have read here. Full medical clearance from a licensed physician should be obtained before beginning or modifying any diet, exercise, or lifestyle program, and your physician should be informed of all nutritional changes.

Table of Contents

Book #1 - Meatless Power Cookbook For Vegan Athletes 8
Vegan Diet and Athletes 9
    What is the vegan diet? 11
    Types of Vegan Diet 11
Basics of a Healthy Vegan Diet 14
    Benefits of a Vegan Diet 15
    Calories 15
    How Do I Track Calories Correctly? 16
    How to Calculate Your Daily Calorie Needs 17
    High-Protein Vegan Food Sources 18
    Proteins 18
    Carbohydrates 19
    Dietary Fats 20
    Macronutrients 21
    How Much Protein Should You Consume as a Vegan? 21
    How Much Fat Should You Consume as a Vegan? 22
    How many Carbs Should You Consume as a Vegan? 22
    Nutrient Timing Explained 23
    Supplements for Vegans 24
Main Vegan Food Categories 26
    Vegetables 26
    Benefits of Beans and Legumes 26
    Benefits of Whole Grains 27
    Benefits of Fruits 27
    Benefits of Berries 28
    Benefits of Nuts and Seeds 28
How to Lose Fat and Build Muscle on a Plant-Based Diet 29
    Muscle Building Formula 29
    Bulking and Cutting 31
    Fat Loss Formula 31
    Cheat Sheets 32
    Pea Protein Powder 33
    How to Use Creatine? 33
    Vegan Food for Energy 34
BREAKFAST 36
    Carrots and Raisins Muffins 37
    Green Protein Tornado Smoothie 39
    Multi Protein Smoothie 40
    Nutty Silken Tofu with Berries Smoothie 41
    Oat - Raspberries Granola 42
    Porridge with Oatmeal and Maca Powder 43
    Savory Potato-Turmeric Pancakes 44
    Sheer Vegan Meatza 45
    Sour Edamame Spread 47
    Spicy Banana, Oat & Coconut Mash 48
    Stamina Tofu "Omelette" 49
    Superelan Vegan Quark Smoothie 50
    The Power of Banana & Soya Smoothie 52

Toasted Tempeh - Vegan Mayo Sandwich 53
Vegan Parsley and Almond Bread 54
Vegan Sloppy Joe with Tofu 55
Vegan Super Green Giant Smoothie 56
Vegan Sweet "French Toast" 57
Vigorous Dragon Fruit Smoothie 58

LUNCH **59**
Asian Chilled Cucumber and Seaweed Soup 60
Baked "Hasselback" Sweet Potatoes 61
Baked Buffalo Cauliflower 'Wings' 62
Baked Creamy Corn with Shredded Tofu 63
Baked Tamari-Tofu and Cabbage Salad 64
High-Protein Minestrone Soup (Crock Pot) 65
Hot Sour and Spicy Bok Choy Salad 66
Integral Rotini Pasta with Vegetables 67
Mushrooms and Chickpeas Risotto 68
Pasta Salad with Marinated Artichoke Hearts and Tofu 69
Raw Creamy Coconut - Curry Soup 70
Slow-Cooked Navy Bean Soup 71
Sour Artichoke Hearts with Rice 72
Spring Greens and Rice Stew 73
Sweet Potatoes Puree with Almond Milk (Slow Cooker) 74
Tomato Soup with Tagliatelle Pasta 75
Vegan Brown Rice Stuffed Zucchini 76
Vegan Pesto Zucchini Noodles 77
Vegan Spaghetti with Soy Sauce 78
White Beans with Herbed Horn Peppers 79

DINNER **80**
Beans and Button Mushrooms "Stew" 81
Boosting Black Beans and Avocado Salad 82
Brown Rice Pasta Salad with Apple Juice Sauce 83
Garlic -Potato Puree 84
High Protein Soybean Pasta with Basil 85
Instant Robust Vegan Soup 86
Instant Savory Gigante Beans 88
Instant Turmeric Risotto 89
Nettle Soup with Rice 90
Okra with Grated Tomatoes (Slow Cooker) 91
Oven-baked Smoked Lentil 'Burgers' 92
Powerful Spinach and Mustard Leaves Puree 94
Quinoa and Rice Stuffed Peppers (oven-baked) 95
Quinoa and Lentils with Crushed Tomato 96
Silk Tofu Penne with Spinach 97
Slow-Cooked Butter Beans, Okra and Potatoes Stew 98
Soya Minced Stuffed Eggplants 99
Triple Beans and Corn Salad 101
Vegan Raw Pistachio Flaxseed 'Burgers' 102
Vegan Red Bean 'Fricassee' 103

SNACKS **104**
Beans with Sesame Hummus 105
Candied Honey-Coconut Peanuts 106
Choco Walnuts Fat Bombs 107

- Crispy Honey Pecans (Slow Cooker) ... 108
- Crunchy Fried Pickles ... 109
- Granola bars with Maple Syrup ... 110
- Green Soy Beans Hummus ... 111
- High Protein Avocado Guacamole ... 112
- Homemade Energy Nut Bars ... 113
- Honey Peanut Butter ... 114
- Mediterranean Marinated Olives ... 115
- Nut Butter & Dates Granola ... 116
- Oven-baked Caramelize Plantains ... 117
- Powerful Peas & Lentils Dip ... 118
- Protein "Raffaello" Candies ... 119
- Protein-Rich Pumpkin Bowl ... 120
- Savory Red Potato-Garlic Balls ... 121
- Spicy Smooth Red Lentil Dip ... 122
- Steamed Broccoli with Sesame ... 123
- Vegan Eggplant Patties ... 124

SWEETS/DESSERTS ... 125

- Beets Bars with Dry Fruits ... 126
- Cocoa, Avocado and Chia Cream ... 127
- Coconut Balls with Lemon Rinds ... 128
- Coconut Rice Pudding with Cardamom ... 129
- Coconutty Cake ... 130
- Dark Honey Hazelnut Cookies ... 131
- Energy Dried Figs Brownies ... 132
- Hearty Apple Bran Muffins ... 133
- Honey Raisins Crispy Balls ... 134
- Protein Banana and Vanilla Cream ... 135
- Protein Carrot Macaroons ... 136
- Raw Lemon 'Cheesecake' ... 137
- Semolina Cake with Brown Sugar Syrup ... 138
- Strawberries, Quinoa and Silk Tofu Dessert ... 139
- Strawberry and Banana Ice Cream ... 140
- Sunrise Peach Marmalade ... 141
- Vegan Blueberry Ice Cream ... 142
- Vegan Hazelnut - Coffee Truffles ... 143
- Vegan Protein - Chocolate Ice Cream ... 144
- Winter Pumpkin Pancakes ... 145
- One Last Thing ... 146

Book #2 - Vegan Meal Prep Cookbook for Athletes ... 147
Meal Prep ... 148

- Follow these meal prep tips: ... 148
- How to properly reheat your refrigerated/frozen food? ... 148

BREAKFAST ... 149

- Almond Queen Fruit Smoothie ... 150
- Baked Raisins & Pumpkin Energy Bars ... 151
- Baked Savory Oat-Apple Bars ... 152
- Boosting Celery-Coconut Smoothie ... 153
- Breakfast Potato Patties ... 154
- Carrot 'Cake' Smoothie ... 155
- Carrot, Almond and Dill Muffins ... 156
- Dark Cacao Banana Muffins ... 157

- Darkwood Coconut Smoothie 159
- Delicious Seasoned Tomato Bread 160
- Frozen Berries Vigor Smoothie 161
- Green Quinoa Breakfast Patties 162
- High Protein Chia and Banana Smoothie 163
- Iced Salad and Pineapple Smoothie 164
- Dried Fruit Energy Bars 165
- Savory Storm White Smoothie 166
- Simple Vegan Waffles 167
- Spicy Vegan Breakfast Smoothie 168
- Total Almond & Ginger Pear Cake 169
- Vegan Spinach Artichoke Quiche with Tofu 170

LUNCH 172

- Aromatic Spinach with Basil-Sesame Puree 173
- Baked Quinoa and Black Beans Patties 174
- Barley and Broccoli Pilaf 175
- Cabbage and Cauliflower Puree 176
- Dark Red Vegan Soup 177
- Delicious Breaded Tofu Sticks 178
- Eggplant and Parsley Puree 179
- Fresh Garden Vegetable Soup 180
- Fried Tofu with Asparagus and Chinese Sauce 181
- Fried Tomato Sauce 182
- Hearty and Creamy Corn Chowder 183
- High-protein Quinoa with Celery and Pine Nuts 184
- Instant Fava Bean Soup with Saffron 185
- Instant Lentils Bolognese 186
- Jasmine Rice and Peas Risotto 187
- Simple Lentil Soup 188
- Oven-baked Peas Fritters 189
- Robust Potato, Rice, and Spinach Soup 190
- Spiced Cabbage, Soybeans and Peanuts Stew 191
- Vegan Potato and Mushroom Frittata 192

DINNER 193

- Artichoke Hearths with Brown Rice 194
- Baked Sweet Potato with Green Beans 195
- Beans and Cauliflower Soup 196
- Beans, Sesame and Pine Nuts Puree 197
- Beluga Lentils and Tofu 'Meatballs' 198
- Black Eyed Beans with Spinach 199
- Eggplants with Peppercorn - Tamari Sauce 200
- Garlic Black Beans and Rice Stew 201
- Gigante Beans and Tomatoes Stew 202
- Greek Ratatouille 203
- Mediterranean Pie Stuffed with Black Olives 204
- Penne with Lemony Asparagus 205
- Quinoa with Vegetables Briam 206
- Roasted Brussels sprouts with Tofu 207
- Roasted Pepper Sauce 208
- Simple Vegan Lasagna with Tofu 209
- Stuffed Bell Peppers with Rice and Pine Nuts 211
- Sweet Red and Black Chili with Cinnamon 212
- Tuscan Kale with Tamari Sauce 213

    Yellow Noodles in Garlic - Hoisin Sauce 214

SNACKS 215

    Banana and Peanut Butter Tortillas 216
    Barbecue Bean Dip (Instant Pot) 217
    Breaded Cauliflower Florets 218
    Coconut- Berry Cream with Turmeric 219
    Creamy Eggplant-Flax Dip 220
    Energy Carob Strawberry Bars 221
    Fragrant Spiced Olives 222
    Fried Chickpeas Cashew Fritters 223
    Ginger-Turmeric Butternut Squash Chips 224
    Homemade Coconut - Vanilla Popcorn 225
    Oat Biscuits with Seeds 226
    Olive Crackers 227
    Oven-baked Kale-Cashews Chips 228
    Pesto Dip with Nuts 229
    Protein Almonds and Carrots Patties 230
    Roasted Cabbage Wedges 231
    Row Pistachio Flaxseed Patties 232
    Seasoned Spinach Patties 233
    Simple Sweet Potato Chips 234
    Soft Cauliflower and Pecans Spread 235

SWEETS/DESSERTS/ENERGYBARS 236

    "Rugged" Coconut Balls 237
    Almond - Choco Cake 238
    Banana-Almond Cake 239
    Banana-Coconut Ice Cream 240
    Coconut Butter Clouds Cookies 241
    Chocomint Hazelnut Bars 242
    Coco-Cinnamon Balls 243
    Express Coconut Flax Pudding 244
    Full-flavored Vanilla Ice Cream 245
    Irresistible Peanut Cookies 246
    Murky Almond Cookies 247
    Orange Semolina Halva 248
    Seasoned Cinnamon Mango Popsicles 249
    Strawberry Molasses Ice Cream 250
    Strawberry-Mint Sorbet 251
    Vegan Choco - Hazelnut Spread 252
    Vegan Exotic Chocolate Mousse 253
    Vegan Lemon Pudding 254
    Vitamin Blast Tropical Sherbet 255
    Walnut Vanilla Popsicles 256
    About the Author 257
    One Last Thing 258

MEATLESS POWER COOKBOOK FOR VEGAN ATHLETES

100 High Protein Recipes to be Muscular and Plant-Based Diet Meal Plans for Beginners

Joseph P. Turner

VEGAN DIET AND ATHLETES

Getting your body in shape requires figuring out the kind of diet you can hold indefinitely. This would most commonly be a diet that's affordable, light on your digestion, and in line with your personal beliefs and lifestyle.

When you add the requirement of achieving athletic results on a vegan diet, you've entered a whole new paradigm of eating that comes down to having a scientifically based and competitive diet that lets you achieve your inner potential to the fullest.

Veganism. You see it all over the place, and lots and lots of people like to talk about it, which, of course, leads to a completely reliable source of information… ha! Wouldn't that be great? But, as humanity kicks in, you start to realize that a lot of these sources are completely untrustworthy.

Now, as more and more people talk about it and more and more opinions get thrown around, mixed in with some fallacies and judgments, combined with some paranoia, and you get yourself a nice, tasty Stew of Ignorance with just a dabble of truth at the bottom, but you can't even see it because of all the stuff floating around on top of it. Don't drink the Stew of Ignorance! Instead, look for real sources who are on the side of the facts (that's me). Through the new chapters, I'll be taking various things out of the Stew of Ignorance until we get to the root of the matter.

The first "ingredient" that mucks up the Stew of Ignorance is myths. Myths, myths, myths. There's about a bazillion of them associated with veganism, but let's knock off each one, one at a time, good and bad, and give you a real picture of what veganism is actually about. Pour out that Stew of Ignorance!

Myth Number 1: The biggest one is that veganism cannot actually sustain you. You've probably heard this argument before, maybe even toted with a "we aren't rabbits, you know." Funny? Yes. But also completely untrue. Now, there is some merit to this argument, and here it is: if you don't do it right, cutting out meat and dairy products can lead to some deficiencies (like vitamin B, calcium deficiencies, etc.). Here's the thing it all boils down to: if you don't plan, no diet will really work. Before starting such a diet, make sure to be knowledgeable about the potential drawbacks and plan for them, thus destroying Myth Number 1.

Myth Number 2: Veganism makes you healthier than normal diets! It's the exact opposite of Myth Number 1, and it's also just... well, it's just not entirely correct. Yes, various studies have shown that people who are vegans tend to have lower rates of heart disease and cancers and actually just feel better in general. On face value, hooray! Veganism fixes everything! The truth is a bit more complicated: most people who are vegans also practice very healthy lifestyles and, once you remove the figures about meat-eaters who skew the data with terrible health (cigarette smokers, overeaters, etc.), there's about the same low rate between vegans and non-vegans. So, yes, if you are a healthy person and you take care of yourself, you will be better off both in the short and long term.

Myth Number 3: Veganism leads to protein deficiencies. Essential amino acids, which, you guessed it, are essential, serve as the building blocks that make up protein. The body can't make them all, so you have to eat them. Yes, many plant proteins have a pretty low number of essential amino acids (which is protein, basically), which would be terrible if you only ate these foods. However, this can be easily bypassed through the use of other plant-based proteins, like rice and beans, nuts, seeds, legumes, etc. In other words, make sure you're not just having one kind of thing and watch what you eat, and you should have no problems with protein deficiencies. There are a lot of myths about not veganism making people tired, weak, etc., but it all is this same thing: combine foods to properly dodge this. We'll be including some meal plans at the end.

Myth Number 4: You can't build muscle on a vegan diet. In reality, the correct factual statement is that you absolutely can gain muscle on a vegan diet, but you have to put more effort into it. Your average person needs 0.4 to 0.5 grams of protein per pound of body weight for general health, but if you're trying to put on muscle, think closer to .8 to 1 gram per pound per day. Can you get that from a vegan diet? Sure, but you are going to have to eat a lot of legumes, nuts, seeds, and might even want to throw in a vegan protein supplement for good measure.

Myth Number 5: You will always lose weight on a vegan diet. Not true, because there's a fundamental formula: unless you expend more calories than you eat, you will not lose weight. The difference here is that with a lot of diets, it's very, very easy to rack up calories. In a vegan diet, many foods are quite low in calories, so you have to eat an awful lot to make up for the calorie density difference. That's why most people when they start vegan diets, end up losing weight: a bunch of legumes the size of a slice of cheesecake is going to have an awful lot less calories (and, of course, that's a pretty big dramatization, but you get my point).

What is the vegan diet?

A vegan diet is a stricter form of the vegetarian diet that mandates eating only non-animal products. While vegetarians may afford themselves some wiggle room to eat something non-vegetarian once in a while, vegans typically don't use any products that contain any ingredients originating from or tested on animals.

A vegan will typically choose this diet because of health, ethical, or environmental reasons. If the person had health problems because of a diet rich in animal foodstuffs or opposes the unethical treatment of animals in the food industry or considers human exploitation of the environment over the top, then the vegan diet is the most appropriate solution.

A vegan diet is most often accompanied by but doesn't necessarily include the idea of toning down on consumerism. In other words, a vegan is an animal lover who rebels against the consumer culture and strikes his own path through the world. In other words, vegan is a hardcore vegetarian.

Pop quiz! Which (vegans or vegetarian) cannot have a fur coat? Answer—vegans! Vegans tend to be a lot more strict about their choices. And now you know. Both nutritionally speaking, often are low in saturated fat and cholesterol while being high in minerals, vitamins, and fibers. Both of the diets required careful meal planning or supplementation to duck the potential deficiencies.

Types of Vegan Diet

So, the aspiring vegan chose to avoid animal-based products but that's the vast majority of food items on the market. Now what? Depending on the person's budget and life circumstances, one subtype of veganism might be more suitable than the other. They will all typically forbid meat, dairy, and eggs but some have a lax set of rules that makes them look more like a vegetarian diet.

RAW FOOD

Thermal processing of foods makes them suitable for human consumption but also destroys valuable nutrients inside; at least that's what the raw food vegan diet claims.

By cooking plant foods at 48 °C (118 °F) or lower and eating only raw fruits, veggies, seeds, and nuts, raw food vegans avoid animal products while staying healthy.

WHOLE FOOD

Just like with the raw food diet, whole food goes for fruits, veggies, seeds, and nuts but eases up restrictions on what packaged goods can be eaten. For example, the raw food will exclusively ask for fresh produce but whole food allows eating packaged goods with less than five ingredients. Keep away from added sugar and mind the additives, though.

80-10-10

Instead of allowing all nuts and seeds, 80-10-10 limits fat intake and mandates soft greens plus raw fruits. This type of vegan diet is most commonly called "fruitarian". The name comes from the idea that 80% of calories should be carbs, 10% protein, and 10% fats. The theory is that humans aren't omnivores but subsisted for millions of years on leafy greens and fruit, which caused our digestion to adapt to those foods.

RAW TILL 4

A derivative of the 80-10-10 diet, "raw till 4" allows for a cooked meal for supper. This diet is mostly a transitional solution for those who have tried going onto a raw or 80-10-10 diet and repeatedly failed. There is some merit to the idea of timing meals but the research is inconclusive and suggests a combination of fasting and hefty meals.

THE STARCH SOLUTION

Another high carb diet like 80-10-10, the starch solution focuses on foods such as potatoes, legumes, corn, and rice rather than fruit. Also known as The McDougall Program, this diet also allows for tofu, yeast, poultry seasoning, egg replacer, and similar non-foods. The purpose of the starch solution is to make the notion of dieting palatable through highly appealing starches that taste sweet on the tongue.

TIP: *Always scan the product's label and packaging. Look for products that have the "Certified Vegan" logo. If the product is simply labeled "vegan" or "contains no animal ingredients" do not take that as a guarantee, read the full ingredient list and find out for yourself.*

THE THRIVE DIET

Professional athlete Brendan Brazier formulated the thrive diet. His book of the same name suggests foods such as apple cider vinegar, brown rice, beans, fruits, rice, and other vegan goodies. Other than that, the diet is most reminiscent of the raw diet and asks for minimally processed (cooked) foods.

JUNK FOOD

When all else fails, it's time for the junk vegan diet. The idea is to eat mock foods devoid of animal products, such as fake meats, mock cheeses and so on. Despite what it might seem like, there is still some value to the junk food diet; it helps people addicted to actual junk food get their fix while weaning them off of it.

BASICS OF A HEALTHY VEGAN DIET

Before we even start here, I want to point out that this will never be a complete guide to everything dieting and nutritional. There's just too much stuff out there to fit into a book like this. However, what we *are* going to do here is give you the most critical factors that will actually affect your health, starting with the most significant thing to focus on and working our way to progressively less important, so pay particular attention at the start.

I also want to point out that none of this is my opinion. I didn't throw open the laptop and get to typing my thoughts. This is a fact, solid, proven fact through various studies and analyses. People much smarter than me have looked at these studies and compiled the five factors that affect the outcome more than the others, the ones that I will share… now.

Calorie balance. The biggest thing that you absolutely need to focus on is this little fella, which is basically how many calories are coming into your body through eating and drinking versus how much energy (measured in calories) is leaving on a regular basis.

Food composition. Aka, what your foods are made of and where your fats, carbs, and proteins come from.

Macronutrient amounts. A big word that just means how much fat, carbs, and protein that you consume on a daily basis.

Nutrient timing. When you eat your meals and (obviously) how you space them out during the day.

Supplements. Notice that this is down here, at number five, despite all the buzz you get around them. These are still important, but here's the basic definition: all those powders, pills, extracts, etc., that you can take to improve your diet.

And that's it! Really. See how relatively simple that is? When you get down to it, it isn't as challenging to wrap your mind around as some of the naysayers like to claim. This should be pretty obvious, but they all affect each other. Changing any of them, or multiple of them can change a lot of stuff. The no-brainer example is that if you eat less, you lose weight. If you happen to be overweight, that means a lot of health benefits.

Look, I want to point out something here. As much as we'd all like a magical pill that could solve all our problems, it doesn't exist. Veganism and eating right might be the right answer and something that makes your life better, but it's baby steps. You don't eat some legumes, and the next day everything's 100% better. If you choose to adopt a vegan diet, I want you to be fully aware that, like with everything else in life, it will take some time. Focus on the most significant things first, like calorie balance, and once things start making sense and you're comfortable, move to the other ones.

Benefits of a Vegan Diet

Animal products carry with them a whole array of health risks, all of which are avoided on a vegan diet, which boasts the following benefits:

- lowered cancer risk
- improved kidney function
- lowered risk of Alzheimer's disease
- reduced arthritis symptoms
- weight loss

Keep in mind that a lot of studies showing these benefits typically have a small sample size. There isn't enough interest in the scientific community to fund large-scale studies of a vegan diet. However, weight loss is the best confirmed and comes about as a result of avoiding saturated fats and animal protein that is responsible for weight gain, especially when combined.

Calories

I'm going to say something here that might make you gasp and turn away in horror. Ready? **Physics.** Yes, physics. If you don't like it, I'm sorry, but it's crucial for your understanding of calories, the enigmatic little fellas themselves. But don't worry, I'll try and keep this understandable and readable.

The First Law of Thermodynamics, for those of us who paid attention to science class, states that your body weight is dependent only on the difference between the amount of calories than you consume versus the amount of calories that you burn (aka, your calorie balance). In other words, your weight is determined by how much you eat versus how many calories you expel doing stuff per day. You can eat a lot, if you do a ton of stuff during the day, and not gain weight. The flip is also true.

But what is a calorie? **A calorie** is the amount of energy required to raise the temperature of one liter of water by one degree Celsius. Gah. Science words again. Here's what you need to know: it's a unit of energy. When you eat, you consume the energy stored within your food. You then have more energy to do things like a frolic in the meadow, workout, or read a book on veganism. Now, in a perfect world, you'd use exactly the amount of energy that you ate each day, but it doesn't always work that way. Most of the time, we eat more calories than we expel, so you have a leftover bunch of calories hanging around after the day is done with nothing to do. Some will go into the muscles and liver as glycogen, but then, when that fills up... it gets stored as fat. The dreaded fat.

Here are the three states of calorie balances. You will only be able to be in one of these states at a time.

Negative calorie balance. Basically, you are not giving yourself enough calories, so you're losing weight. You might have a very high activity rate or something like that, but if you are expelling more calories than you are gaining, this will make you drop some pounds. This might sound great, but be careful: the necessary energy you absolutely need won't just appear: it'll come from the breakdown of body tissue.

Neutral calorie balance. You did it. You nailed it right on the head. You have eaten exactly the amount of calories that you need each day, which means you will not gain or lose weight. If you haven't changed weight in a few months, congratulations, you're in neutral calorie balance!

Positive calorie balance. This is where most of us get into trouble: we're eating too many calories and not doing enough to get rid of them, so we start stacking on the weight. The calories that we don't end up using are stored as fat or glycogen in the liver and muscles.

Calories can be confusing to a lot of people because if you aren't eating enough, you won't gain muscles... but eat incorrectly, and you'll be gaining fat, not muscle. If you just aren't eating enough, you will not be able to put on any muscle even though you have very low body fat. It's a tightrope, but fortunately for everyone, it isn't that hard of a tightrope to walk down once you get the hang of it.

How Do I Track Calories Correctly?

Did you notice that I put the word "correctly" on there? Yeah, that's there for a reason. There are a billion ways to track calories, but none of them will help you if you aren't doing it right. If this seems confusing to you, you aren't alone. Many people find this hard to do, and most of the apps and programs are incredibly unintuitive, complicated, or full of ads that make it a nightmare. It can actually be pretty simple. Here, I'll be sharing with you a suite of strategies and tools that you can use and, just as importantly, which foods actually need to be tracked and which you can safely ignore.

Get out your checklist, because you're going to need three, count 'em, three things for this. The first is the food. Duh. Second is a calorie tracker app (try out Fitatu, which is free in the app store), and your basic kitchen scale, which doesn't have to be terribly expensive. Think less than $40 range. Some people try and do this without a scale, but that's just not realistic for beginners. I'm sure that some scientists don't need a calculator, but for the vast majority of us, you might as well make it easy instead of instantly making it difficult. Eyeballing, it takes skill and practice, and getting off can screw up the whole plan.

Here's how it works. First, throw your food (not literally) on the scale and get the right amount in terms of grams, so you know how many calories you'll be getting from it. This is actually important, so you need to make sure to do two things:

First, you're going to make sure that your macro and calorie counter is accurate. Second, you're going to need to be smart about it and not bog yourself down all the time. Streamline! Here's the five-point system for getting your scale to do these two things. Okay? Let's do it!

First, you really don't need to sweat the small stuff. Consider anything under 50 calories to not be worth counting, in general. Some coffee might fall into this category or some cream. Minor things. This isn't meant to be horrible, but it will be if you of every single thing down to that level. The important thing is to keep it reasonable. Adding up a bunch of these tiny items can make a big difference.

Second, just weigh the food once. For example, if you eat oatmeal frequently, just measure what you need in a day for the oatmeal in a bowl. The next day, you don't have to carefully measure out everything unless you want to, because you should be able to accurately eyeball what you need for oatmeal. Sure, knock yourself out and weigh everything every day, but I'm telling you—it isn't going to make as much difference as you might be worried.

Third, you need to know if your food is raw or cooked because it makes a difference for calories. If you weigh rice before and after the water goes into it, it's going to be enormously different. Anything that might affect the weight should be considered, like a banana peel throwing off the scale.

Fourth, check the macro and calorie values in your tracker app. Just because it's in the app does not mean it is accurate. If you think a value might be off, just check with something like Web M.D. to make sure. Yes, it really does happen. You don't want to mess up your diet because your values are wrong.

Fifth, you only really need the food scale for one-off occasions. Meal plans are the best way to do things since they are more reliable and easier, and since they are recurring, you will find yourself not needing your food scale all the time after a while. This means that you will eventually need the food scale for stuff you are not too familiar with.

How to Calculate Your Daily Calorie Needs

Well, we're past the definitions! It's actually not that difficult, right? The calorie balance is the thing that will make or break your diet, and you can either be in positive, negative, or neutral calorie states. Which state are you in right now? You might not know. The only way to truly know which state that you are in is to know how many calories your body spends every day. Since you can't just ask your body this question, you're going to need to use formulas. And, like all formulas, some are easier than others, and some are more accurate than others.

The easiest way is to calculate your TDEE, which is a fancy way of describing your total daily energy expenditure (how many calories you burn in a day). The way you calculate is by estimating the number of calories you burn while resting, which is known as the basal Metabolic Rate, aka BMR. Then, once you know that number, you throw on an estimated number of calories that you burn through how often you exercise.

Unless you happen to be a genius, you won't know what your TDEE is off-hand. Never to fear! You can follow this here link, and it will do all the work for you.

(https://tdeecalculator.net/)

It's gonna ask you for various stats, like height, weight, age, and activity. It's not going to be 100% accurate, seeing as nobody is exactly alike, but you just need an estimate, and it should be close. Do you think the TDEE calculator is off? No worries. Here's how to test it. Use the estimated TDEE value and eat how many calories it recommends per day. Weigh yourself twice a week, and if something changes, it's off. If you start gaining weight, decrease the TDEE by 100 calories. If you keep gaining weight, do it again. The same goes for the opposite. Losing weight? Add 100 calories a day. You want to find that perfect TDEE where you are not gaining or losing weight.

High-Protein Vegan Food Sources

Without getting all technical on you, it's crucial to eat the right food. How many calories you eat is first and foremost, but this is a close second. There are four factors of food sources that you're going to need to consider, which are protein sources, carbohydrate sources, fat sources, and micronutrients. I'll be going over each. Now, I want to point out that your diet must work for you. If you absolutely despise a certain kind of food, don't have it in your diet. Find another alternative, or your diet will probably not last all that long. However, if I had to give you four bullet points to live by as a vegan, it's this.

- Get most of your protein from foods high in essential amino acids
- Get most of your carbs from whole grains, fruits, and veggies
- Get most of your fats from sources of unsaturated fat
- Eat foods mostly high in vitamins and minerals

Without further ado, let's get into the science of it all!

Proteins

Proteins are crucial. I literally could not go over all the scientific reasons you need protein, but I'll say it this way: if you don't have the right protein, you basically fall apart. Things go real bad, real fast. That's why it's so important to nail it.

For the workout enthusiasts, you'll need to know this: protein is responsible for building new muscles, and it's what prevents your current muscles from going away. Most (90%) of the protein you eat gets turned into amino acids, which becomes part of the amino acid pool that your body will use to build or repair muscle or other tissues. Carbs and fat can be stored for later use, but amino acids cannot, so you need to have protein every day. Remember the bit about essential amino acids from earlier? Like I said there, you're going to need to get them from somewhere because your body can't make them.

How to find quality vegan protein sources

The title gives it away, but you need quality vegan protein sources. There are several ways that you can measure the quality of a vegan protein source, including the concept of bioavailability, which is a complicated word that literally just means how much of the protein you consume actually ends up getting absorbed into your bloodstream. You could also judge protein quality based on how much of the protein is composed of those essential amino acids (and how much is non-essential amino acids, which your body can make and doesn't need to get from food). Tragically for veganism, animal protein sources are usually regarded as better because they are better digested and have a higher percentage of essential amino acids than plant-based proteins. Fortunately for veganism, this is not generally a problem. There are a few exceptions, including a fruit-only diet, which probably is a poor decision, and people trying to build up muscle.

If you're a run of the mill vegan that does not fall into those subcategories, you should be fine from pumpkin seeds, chia seeds, oats, lentils, kidney beans, black beans, mung beans, and peanuts. A lot of beans. There are others, of course, but these are some great ones to consider.

If you are a person trying to build muscle, fret not! I'll explain that in more detail later.

Carbohydrates

Carbs are the last of the three main macronutrients. There's quite a bit of argument over carbs, but first, let's figure out what they actually are. They're found in foods including vegetables, whole grains, pastries, candy, potatoes, and fruits. They're often considered the body's preferred energy source. It's extremely important for all parts of your life and, like protein, has a variety of reasons as to why. One vital thing is that **carbs supply the nervous system with its fuel**, for lack of a better term. That means more fatigue resistance, more workout motivation, and better muscle recruitment. A lot of the fatigue-related to long-duration training is linked to this, so you have to give your nervous system enough of a source of blood glucose to keep things up and running smoothly.

Carbs refuel glycogen stores. Glycogen is a provider of energy for high-intensity workouts, but it also stores in the muscle and plays a hand in muscle growth. If you want to get more muscle, you need to give yourself enough carbs.

Carbs secrete insulin. Eat more carbs, secrete more insulin. That's great, seeing as insulin has a profound effect on muscle growth. I could give you a long and complicated explanation as to why, but I'll keep it short: insulin helps muscle tissue grow.

How to find quality vegan carbohydrate sources

Look for unprocessed whole foods, like legumes, whole grains, many veggies, and fruit, oh wonderful fruit. They contain vitamins, minerals, antioxidants, and fiber. Avoid foods made with refined grains, as they have less of these nutrients, and duck anything with sugar thanks to unnecessary calories. For high carb whole grain sources, look for whole-grain pasta, whole-grain cereal, whole grain bread, and more—but avoid the sugar. For high carb fruits, look for apples, oranges, pears, mangos, and bananas. For high carb legumes, look for peas, beans, and lentils. Some other good options that I haven't gone over are sweet or long-duration potatoes, normal and brown rice, canola or meal, and tortillas.

Dietary Fats

I'd be willing to bet that you hear more rumors about this one than any other, largely because it has the word "fat" in it, which is often associated with something unhealthy. Well, I'll tell you right now that you shouldn't read into that too much because you need some dietary fats. Without going into the science of it, they're crucial. They fit in a lot of important things, from helping you absorb vitamins to regulate hormone production, make your hair and skin look good, and more. It's important, and not "bad like was previously believed.

Now, there is some credence to avoiding foods with a lot of saturated fats. Think cheese, whole milk, ice cream, fatty meats, butter, that kind of thing. There's a debate about it and what it does with your risk of heart problems, but as of now, from me to you, I'd just try and keep a limit on foods high with saturated fats. Unsaturated fats? They can actually lower your LDL cholesterol (something you want). Within this, there are monounsaturated fats, which include canola oil and olive oil, and then there are polyunsaturated fats, which include soy oil and sunflower corn. Trans fatty acids (formed by infusing vegetable oil with hydrogen) helps keep food fresh for a more extended time. Sound great? Well, not exactly, as studies have shown that a pretty small amount of them can increase your risks of various problems, like heart disease and depression, and obviously, you don't want that. What's the solution? Avoid (or limit) food with partially hydrogenated oils and hydrogenated oils (margarine and hard butter, for example).

Basically, you've got three categories of fat: **unsaturated, saturated, and trans fats.** I'll be explaining each, briefly.

Unsaturated fats can actually be broken down into monounsaturated fats and polyunsaturated fats—which are healthy fats and should be included in your diet because they have excellent health benefits. You need fat, okay? It all boils down to that. No matter what your neighbor says, a healthy person *needs* to have some fun to function. Think 15 to 25 percent of all daily calories. Of this, you should get most of that from your unsaturated fats. Turn to your old pals—avocados, olives, olive oil, nuts and butter (but not highly processed kinds), flaxseed oil, flax seeds, and many other types of seeds. Good? Good.

Then, we have **saturated fats.** They're easily found in animal products like butter, cheese, dairy, fatty steaks, etc. They often play the villain in media, but in reality, they're not as bad as they're supposed to be. Now, you should absolutely limit your consumption of saturated fats, but vegans don't consume any of the things I just mentioned, so a vegan already does that.

Trans fats. Like transformers, but less interesting. They're the Frankenstein of fats, as they're made by adding hydrogen to liquid vegetable oils, which makes them more solid and less... liquidy. The point is that this will increase the shelf life of many processed foods. Now, the other ones are kind of grey, but trans fats are actually bad for your health, so avoid these. Want to know where you find these most often? Fast food, fried food, and more. Yeah. That's why you should avoid them.

Macronutrients

The first thing that you need to focus on is your calorie balance, but number two is macronutrients. They are, simply put, the three main ingredients that you need to survive. The three macronutrients are carbs, dietary fat, and proteins. We just went over these, so I won't spend too much time here. Instead, I'll jump straight into what you really need to know.

How Much Protein Should You Consume as a Vegan?

Remember the thing about protein deficiencies with a vegan diet? Well, that can absolutely be a thing, but here's the fun part: it's only a problem if you let it be a problem. You need protein to gain muscle, period. How much? Well, high protein diets work the best, with .08 to 1 gram/lb of body weight. Let's say that you're just an average, active person who would like to see some muscle gains, but that's not your entire priority. In that case, you're looking at less protein. Your bare minimum would be 0.3 grams/lb per day, but for most folks, this translates to about 40 grams of protein a day—something very attainable.

I want to point out that that is the minimum, and it won't hurt to go over that. Shoot for a higher value, like 0.4 to 0.5. That's particularly important if you're a vegan or vegetarian, seeing as plant-based protein sources are generally digested less efficiently. So, eat more protein than your meat-eating friends to make up for this little fact.

But... can you eat too much protein? Well, yes and no. It's not likely. You'd have to try hard to eat too much of it, especially if you stick to unprocessed or minimally processed, quality sources, and if your higher protein intake doesn't end up lowering your carb and fat intakes to a critical level. Keep it balanced, in other words. There are studies showing kidney and various health problems from high protein diets, that's usually because the participant had preexisting problems or if they were also eating a lot of processed foods and saturated fats. Don't read too much into that, as fears around protein shakes are pretty unfounded generally speaking. Do keep in mind that if you do have a lot of protein in your diet, make sure to drink plenty of water.

How Much Fat Should You Consume as a Vegan?

0.3 grams of fat per pound of fat-free mass per day. That's everything that isn't fat, so bone, muscle, and water, basically. This translates to 15 to 20 percent of your daily calories for your average person. You shouldn't try to undercut this when dieting to lose weight and build muscle. Now, it does completely matter what kinds of fat you consume, as we talked about earlier. Avoid saturated fats, artificial trans fats, and instead, focus on monounsaturated and polyunsaturated fats. Most vegan diets do this already, so you should be good. Just make sure to limit your consumption of highly processed "junk" foods, but c'mon, that's pretty obvious.

And can you have too much fat? Well, it depends. You should watch every kind except for monounsaturated fats, like avocados or olive oil, for most vegan diets. Here's a fact—monounsaturated fats, even when you eat a lot of them, are very healthy. It's proven through the Mediterranean diet.

How many Carbs Should You Consume as a Vegan?

Carbs are the only non-essential macronutrient, so, in theory, there's no real minimum regarding general health. You could absolutely survive without any carbs, but this is not a good idea. Some athletes chronically dip too low in carbs and it will show with poor workout performance, poor indirect and direct muscle growth, and more fatigue over days and weeks due to glycogen depletion. In other words, if you don't have carbs, you won't grow as much muscle as you could.

The precise amount of carbs you need depends on a few things. We're talking blood tests, and that sucks. Luckily, you can narrow it down to the range you should have, even without knowing your exact measurements, using bodyweight and training intensity. Here's how!

Ideal Carb Intake:
- Light workouts: 1-1.25g per pound
- Moderate workouts: 1.25-1.5g per pound
- Hard workouts: 1.5-1.75g per pound

In other words, you need more carbs for harder training. Light workouts are usually anything thirty minutes or less and with less than 10 working sets if you're lifting weights; moderate is anything between 30 and 60 minutes and more than 10 working sets; hard workouts are anything above that. It isn't an exact science, but it's pretty close. Sometimes, a short workout can be extremely high in intensity, and if that's you, you might want to bump your carb intake up to the "hard" category.

Can you eat too many carbs? That's a hard question, and I'd be willing to bet that you've heard all the horrible, scary myths about carbs holding you back, but here's the actual truth: there's no real science that can prove an excessive carb intake as long as minimal protein and fat intakes are met. There are actually studies from endurance runners and such that prove very high carb diets can be healthy in the long term, but you have to get your carbs from healthy sources, like oats, potatoes, quinoa, and rice (these are complex carbs that don't make a sudden spike in insulin levels like candy or sugar might).

Some people don't function well with high carb diets, and that's fine. Everyone's different. If that's you, keep the carbs at the bullet points above and put more calories through healthy fats.

Nutrient Timing Explained

Meal timing, one of the most controversial topics in the fitness community. Basically, what we're talking with meal timing is when, exactly, you eat throughout the day. There's meal frequency when is how often you should eat compared to your activity. Is this important? Somewhat, but be wary: lots of beginners, in particular, overestimate its importance.

You should be focusing on macronutrients and calorie balance. If you only focus on those, you should be completely fine. Yes, you could make an argument about the timing, but it can't make or break your diet. Good news for anyone who has a busy lifestyle and can't perfectly plan your meals.

There is something that I want to touch on here: **pre and post-workout nutrition,** which actually does improve workout performance and recovery—especially if your pre and post-workout meals are high in carbs and protein. Remember how I said that protein can't be stored? Yeah, that's why this helps: when you're working your body, and your body needs protein, if it can't find any in the digestive tract, it turns to your muscles and breaks them down for vital functions, which, obviously, you don't want. That's why having a constant supply of protein while working out is important… if you're trying to build mass. If you're not focused on that, you don't really need to worry too much about this.

Myths. So, so many myths about this, so many, in fact, that I can't go over all of them. I will bust down a few for you. Research shows that eating a bunch of tiny meals during the day compared to eating one big meal actually makes no difference to metabolic rates, despite what your local gym buddies might tell you. Breakfast is also not the most important meal of the day. Neither is dinner, or lunch, or anything else. If something tells you that one particular meal is the most important meal of the day and if you miss it, it will be devastating to your health, it's just not true. Yes, you can eat carbs at night. It's not like your body cares when you eat, as long as you get the right amounts. The only time that there is an aberration is the pre and post workouts that I mentioned earlier because science actually supports it.

If this all sounds complex, don't worry. I got you. Here are some scientifically based recommendations for your meal plans for your average person.

Start with 3-6 meals per day. Feel free to include snacks as long as they fit into your total calorie and macro split.

To avoid cravings, spread the meals throughout the day. There's a good reason that humans have traditionally had breakfast, lunch, and dinner with snacks in between. It just works. If you're a person that gets hungry before bed, make dinner later to cover yourself.

Monitor your individual feelings of hunger and adjust accordingly. Not a person hungry in the morning? Not a big deal. Just eat more later.

Supplements for Vegans

The final thing on our list for a healthy diet are supplements. Can supplements replace proper diet planning and nutrition? No, but that doesn't meant they're not useful, particularly if you can get nutrients from them that are hard to find elsewhere. Also, if you're a traveler, they can make your life easier.

Walk into your nearest store and look at the supplements there, long, long lines of different ones that all claim to be incredibly vital, and this and that. It's intimidating, and weird, and confusing to make sense of what's actually important and what's just a marketing gimmick. I know. I've been there. Here's the thing: the supplement industry is enormous. Like, billions of dollars enormous, so these companies will often do anything to get you to buy their product, even if it means stretching the truth or straight-up lying to you. Some are completely worthless. Here's what you should actually look for to avoid giving your hard-earned money for a lie.

Vitamin D. It's great in, well, pretty much everything, but your primary source of this is from sun exposure, so if you live in a place with not a lot of sun exposure or if you just don't go outside too often, this can lead to deficiencies. Is this you? I recommend supplementing with a 1000-2000 IU, which stands for international units of vitamin D per day.

Zinc. It helps the body's immune system, but our bodies don't have a specialized storage system for it, so you should consume zinc every day. Most people get enough zinc from their diet supplementing, but if you have a weak immune system (you get sick a lot), or if you have acne or other skin problems, consider supplementing it, especially in combination with vitamin C. Stay under 40 mg/day. Too much zinc can be toxic longterm.

Omega 3 Fatty Acids. They're found in fish oil usually, but you can find them in vegan alternatives like flaxseed oil. They help with healthy bone grown, maintain strong ligaments, and help maintain healthy cholesterol levels.

Want more information? Great! Here's a free (yes, really free) **Bonus Book,** which you can download at no additional charge, where it goes into more detail for supplements for specific situations, like when you want to boost your immune system further or want to avoid specific deficiencies that are common among vegans.

MAIN VEGAN FOOD CATEGORIES

Vegetables

Veggies! Love them or hate them, you need them in any healthy diet. They're jam-packed with minerals and vitamins while staying remarkably low in calories. They have no cholesterol to boot. They'll help your immune system, digestive system, skeletal system, cardiovascular health, and blood pressure, not to mention that they'll give you healthier skin and hair. As if that wasn't enough, they have high levels of antioxidants, which can keep the growth of cancer cells in check, especially for cruciferous veggies like broccoli. Leafy green vegetables like spinach are high in quercetin, which helps with allergies while being an anti-inflammatory. Green, yellow, and orange vegetables are full of calcium, potassium, iron, and magnesium—which are all minerals that many people are deficient in, particularly athletes.

Fiber. Nature's broom. Crucial for proper digestion and a whole sleuth of other important benefits. It comes in two kinds: insoluble and soluble. You can find both in most veggies. There's a lengthy scientific explanation of what happens to the two kinds and why you need it, but for our purposes, let's stick with the basics: you need your daily dose of fiber, and you can count on your pal vegetables for coming through on that front. Also, because of its volume, fiber makes you feel full faster... without contributing to your calorie balance, which means that you can lose weight faster. It's incredibly difficult to overeat with vegetables, which is why they're a part of so many fat loss diets. It's kind of a win-win scenario to eat them.

Benefits of Beans and Legumes

Lots. Just... lots. Here's a study: eating only one daily serving, around ¾ of a cup, can reduce LDL cholesterol by up to 5 percent while including about 10 to 15 grams of fiber, which is close to your entire daily recommended intake. It helps stabilize blood sugars, giving you a steady supply of energy. They're a staple in all kinds of diets, but they're often overlooked for some reason. You don't have to prepare them. Just go buy yourself the low sodium variety, rinse as much of the salt off as you can, and voila, you get the majority of macro and micronutrients of fresh beans without having to actually prepare them. Also, check out Dried Lentils, which are not only faster to cook (20 to 30 minutes), they don't have sulfur, so don't worry about getting gassy from them.

Benefits of Whole Grains

Controversy, controversy everywhere. Studies and studies both argue for and against eating grains, but most of the bad flak comes from eating refined grains, which are found in junk foods. Whole grains, unlike refined grains, they have all the original components of grain and are, thus, a completely different story. They are the exact opposite of their vilified cousin, the refined grains, and come with lots of legitimate health benefits. They have lots of fiber, both soluble and insoluble, which helps digestion and overall health. A half-cup of uncooked brown rice, for example, will get you 5.5 grams of fiber—a fifth of what you need for the whole day. They can help lower cholesterol and triglycerides, which helps cardiovascular health. Studies have proven that eating two to three servings of whole-grain products per day is much less likely to have heart attacks. Thanks to their high fiber and volume, they're great at weight control without adding much to your calorie balance.

Whole grains are healthy for most folks, but be careful. Some people are not a good fit with whole grains, namely those with celiac disease and gluten sensitivities. Gluten is a type of protein in wheat barley, which some people are allergic to, allergies that can cause fatigue indigestion or overall dizziness. If this is you, go with gluten-free whole grains like rice, oat, and buckwheat.

Benefits of Fruits

Not only are fruits delicious, but they serve crucial functions in your health. They're jam-packed full of minerals and vitamins while being low in calories and high in dietary fiber. Don't cook them, as that makes them lose much of their nutrient content, so each them fresh, ripe, and raw. They're also excellent at instant energy supply, so they are fantastic snacks. I'll say it this way: if it helps your body, a fruit probably does it.

Should you limit your fruit intake because of fructose content? Fructose is a simple carbohydrate and can spike your blood sugar, but that pretty much only happens when it's added to processed foods. In actual fruits, the absorption of fructose will always be delayed thanks to the regulating powers of fiber. I'd recommend steering clear of fruit juices, as they can be extremely high in calories and can spike your blood sugar.

Benefits of Berries

One of the things on here that pretty much everyone can agree on is that berries are amazing. One incredible function is that they primarily benefit your memory and mental fitness, which is why they help fight Alzheimer's disease. The reason that they're so amazing can be boiled down to three things.

Antioxidants. They include vitamins like E, A, and C, which protect cells from damage and possibly from disease.

Resveratrol. They're found in grapes, a few other berries, red wine, and dark chocolate. It may help lower inflammation, prevent clogger arteries, and offers cancer protection.

Flavanoids, which give berries their colors, may help to protect against inflammation, heart disease, and cancer.

Combine these three, and you've got lots of health improvements. The fiber in them slows how fast food moves through your GI tract, which makes you less hungry as an extra benefit as if the other things weren't good enough.

Benefits of Nuts and Seeds

Want better hair and skin? Nuts and seeds. Want better heart health and lower blood pressure. Nuts and seeds. Want high protein content? Nuts and seeds. Want lots of important minerals like magnesium, zinc, calcium, and phosphorous? Nuts and seeds. Want a lowered chance of diabetes? Nuts and seeds. Want omega 3 fatty acids and, therefore, better brain health? Nuts and seeds. Really. There's not a big downside to nuts and seeds, and there are so so many benefits. They're like the superfood, with various kinds sporting particular specialties. Also, bonus points for being delicious a lot of the time.

HOW TO LOSE FAT AND BUILD MUSCLE ON A PLANT-BASED DIET

For this section, let's put away all myths, prejudices (both pro and con), and legends. Let's talk nutritionally because that's the only way that actually matters. Sound good? Okay, we're going to not talk about your specific training regiment here. This is strictly nutrition.

Your body needs certain diet requirements to build muscle, duh. The most important is a *small* calorie surplus and enough protein. When you workout, you will damage your muscles, and these two factors will help your body repair your muscle tissue in a stronger way than it was before. For muscle growth, your protein intake should be between 0.8 and 1 grams/lb of body weight per day. You can absolutely get this through a vegan diet, but you're going to need to be clever. We've already gone over the reasoning behind this, so I'll keep it brief here and give you some examples you can use today.

Peanuts *(26g of protein per 100g)*, mung beans *(24g of protein per 100g)*, kidney beans *(24g of protein per 100g)*, black beans *(21g of protein per 100g)*, chickpeas *(19g of protein per 100g)*, pumpkin seeds *(19g of protein per 100g)*, chia seeds *(17g of protein per 100g)*, oats *(17g of protein per 100g)* and lentils *(9g of protein per 100g)*.

Eat a few servings of those through the day, and you'll get a significant amount of protein very quickly. I'd recommend also tossing in a vegan protein powder supplement, the best of which are usually pea or rice protein powder. Better yet, get one that blends both. Take one or two scoops of them per day, and you'll be fine.

Keep an eye on your calorie balance. You're going to need a slight calorie surplus to gain muscle, which might be difficult, seeing as vegan diets are not known for their ability to let someone overeat. If you're having trouble and find yourself not gaining weight consistently, consider increasing your fat intake through olive oil, which is more calorie-dense than most vegan sources of carbs or protein. If you do this, make sure you still reach your macro requirements of carbs and protein per day.

Here's the bottom line: **you can build muscle and strength on a vegan diet.**

Muscle Building Formula

There are a million books out there about bodybuilding because there's enough information for a million books about bodybuilding. You might have read a few of them, or you've found one of those fitness gurus or magazines that give you all sort of complex hacks and workouts that makes it mighty confusing.

There's just so much information out there. I know, I've looked into it. It makes something that really isn't all that complex seem like rocket science. Here's the great news: if you're not a professional bodybuilder, you don't actually need to know everything. In fact, you need to know precisely three things, these three things that I'll tell you right now.

Train.

Eat.

Recover.

Let's go over that one more time for the people in the back. Train. Eat. Recover. Really. It's that simple. That's literally all you need to do to build muscle. I'll go a little deeper into each of these, but this is exactly as hard as it needs to be.

Train. For workouts, I'd recommend compound exercises/compound movements. Basically, instead of working for just one muscle group, you work many, including many that you just can't with other exercises. You can lift more weight—but be safe—and you'll get faster growth. The biggest of these are the barbell squat, the bench press, the military press, and the deadlift. They're best with heavyweight *within reason* and with fewer reps. I'll be calling these the big four because there are exactly four of them and I'm clever like that.

You're going to see an increase of strength right of the bat because your muscles will be completely surprised by these four. Great! Then, you'll plateau. Don't panic. That's exactly what is expected. It happens to everyone. When that happens, you're going to need to come up with a workout plan that enables you to get stronger when adding more weight isn't an option. Just to confirm, the very much incorrect option is to overload yourself and injure yourself. I can't even begin to emphasize how important it is to do these big four with proper form and safety.

Cardio. Personally, I hate cardio with regarding passion even though it does great stuff for you, but you need to decide what your workout goals are before doing cardio. Cardio burns calories, and if you burn too much, you won't have a that important calorie surplus, and your body just can't build muscle. If you want to pack on muscle, consider eating more or doing less cardio.

Eat. Yes, I know that people like to think of calories as awful, but you need that surplus if you're going to build muscle. Your muscles don't grow as you workout. They grow after you finish, and you need to be getting the right calories and from the right places.

Recover. The fun part for many people this is the part when your body is reeling from working out, getting the necessary fuel, and doing what you want: getting stronger and building muscle. Much of this is done when you sleep, so make sure to get seven to nine hours of uninterrupted sleep per night, at least. Less than seven, and you'll be sacrificing possible progress and maybe your health in general. It'd be pretty stupid to go through all the effort of working out, then lose it because you didn't do the easiest thing on the planet: sleep.

Bulking and Cutting

Lots of bodybuilders and athletes do this. It's two phases, bulking and cutting. Bulking is getting bigger and gaining lots of muscle and size from eating more calories, then cutting is when you try to get rid of this extra body fat by cutting calories while maintaining lean muscle mass. This actually does work, and it's a legitimate thing I would strongly consider if I was you. There's a good reason that people do this. Luckily, it's easy. Lift heavy and eat lots of calories, and you'll grow. If you don't lift heavy enough (and this varies by person), or if you don't eat enough, even if you go to the gym five times a week, this won't work.

If you're a complete beginner, your body will do both cutting and bulking at the same time because it's such a new thing. Once you get more muscle, you will have to focus more on these two actual phases. Now, I want to tell you one thing right now: *don't use any meal plans from the internet.* Many of them are complete garbage that will actually damage you more than helping you. Here's how you do it: calculate your TDEE, then add a certain percentage of your TDEE to get your ideal calorie count for your bulk. Then, get there by eating healthy. Don't decide that you need extra calories and go eat ice cream to get there.

What's the percentage? You'll hear both sides, with some saying to add ten percent and some saying that won't make any difference. The truth lies somewhere in the middle. If you eat way, way over your level, your body won't be able to put all those extra calories towards muscle growth, and you'll get fatter. I'd try 20%, personally. I can't tell you exactly, because this boils down to your individual metabolism. You might have to play with it a bit. If you're a skinnier person with an extremely high metabolism, you're going to need to eat more than a bigger person.

Fat Loss Formula

Right now, google fat loss diets. I'll wait. You'll find eight hundred different, super muscular, super-fit gurus telling you that all the other diets are frauds and only theirs will work, and, what's more, it'll work in no time! Yeah... right. Don't just blindly trust these people. If you want to lose weight, it's very simple. There was actually a study done where people ate literally nothing other than Twinkies and they lost weight because they ate fewer calories than they expended. Heck, if you wanted, you could lose all kinds of weight by literally just not eating, but that's not a good plan, because it's very unhealthy.

No, what you want is not to shrivel up, but to keep your healthy mass and lose fat. There's a big difference here. If you want to do it the healthy way, look at the total calorie count, sure, but look at what's actually in there. You need healthy fats, proteins, and carbs for this to work. You need to also work out during this period, or you will lose muscle along with fat.

Well, hold on, you say. I met this guy who swore he had a diet that could make him gain crazy amounts of muscle and lose all his body fat at *the same time!* Isn't that great? No, no, it is not because that guy is lying to you. Such a thing does not exist.

Ooh, here we go again, with another myth! **The spot reduction myth.** Have fat around your belly that you don't like Well, it would make sense that working on ab exercises would make belly fat go around faster than a chest exercise, right? Unfortunately, no, though that would be awesome. Some people lose fat faster than others in various places, and that's due to a little something called good genes, not the exercises they do. Another myth is that cardio will make you lose weight, which is sometimes true. If you're eating thousands of more calories than you should, you can do all the exercise you want, and you won't lose weight. You'll be putting it on.

You're going to need, for the cutting phase, a calorie deficit. You calculate this the exact same way you calculated the bulking diet, but with a difference. Obviously, you aren't going to add calories on top to lose weight. There are three classifications of calorie deficits:

- Small (10 to 15 percent below your TDEE)
- Moderate (20 to 25 percent below your TDEE)
- Large (More than 25 percent below your TDEE)

Some say that small is good. Others say that moderate is best. Very few say the large is a good plan. If you want to lose body fat fast, a moderate deficit of 20 percent below is probably your best option. If you have a faster metabolism, a smaller deficit will probably do the same thing while you sacrifice less strength while allowing you to eat more during your day. **You need protein while cutting.** Want to lose fat and not muscle? Protein. Normally, it's 0.8-1 gram of protein per pound of body weight.

Cheat Sheets

If you wanna spark an argument in your fitness and nutrition groups, bring up cheat sheets. Basically, let's say that you've been eating healthy for a week, but you really, really want to sneak in that chocolate bar at the end of the week. That's a cheat meal. It doesn't fall into your normal diet, but you really want it as a reward. Is it going to destroy you? No, of course not—as long as you keep your calories and macros in check.

I'm going to go ahead and say that 10 to 20 percent of your diet can be coming from whatever food you want, as long as it fits your total daily calories and proteins, carbs, and fats. Some people, and I've met several, can stick to a 100 percent diet. I can't. I know I can't. I would go insane. Most people would. You aren't a machine. As long as you stick to the basics of correct dieting, cheat meals are not going to cause you to get fat or lose muscle magically. Now, here's your test: you've been eating good, so you decide to eat an entire gallon of ice cream. Was that a good idea? Of course not, because you've gone way over your calorie balance.

And then, there are cheat days. Cheat days are a significantly worse idea than cheat meals because they can actually screw up the plan. If you eat five hundred calories less than your normal every day for a week, great. You can blow it all by eating badly for a day. It's just not worth it. None of us are machines, and it can be tempting to have cheat days, but you'll be shooting yourself in the foot. There are two ways to get around this problem: first, suffer. Second, make a diet that you can stick to.

Pea Protein Powder

Pea powder is made of dried yellow field pieces of fiber as a legume. It contains all the essential amino acids (except for methane). It's an excellent protein source for vegans and vegetarians. It's basically the vegan alternative to whey protein. You need protein for building muscle, and while you can get it from various foods, it's tricky and requires a good amount of planning and calculation... Or you could use pea protein powder with a balanced diet. It's completely vegan, and it's a high-quality protein and is extremely comparable to whey protein, and studies can prove it. Also, since it's not made from milk, it's an excellent choice for those who are lactose intolerant.

Don't use any kind of protein powder as your sole source of protein. Maybe get a third of your diet, a half max, of your protein from protein shakes.

Are there side effects? Nope. It's very safe. If you have preexisting kidney problems, talk to your doctor first, but studies have shown it's safe for everyone else.

How to Use Creatine?

Creatine stands out as one of the very few supplements that actually does make you see more gains. Through the magic of science, it will make you stronger, and it will cause more water retention in your muscles, which you want because it makes them appear bigger and fuller. But, who cares if it isn't safe? Luckily for us, study after study shows that it's completely safe.

But what kind? There are tons of forms, but luckily, the research is pretty obvious: creatine monohydrate is the most effective form. You'll see more expensive kinds, like creatine ethyl and Ke Alkalyn (aka, buffered creatine), but they don't have any extra benefits, and they can be more than twice the price. No, here's what you have to do—traditional creatine monohydrate supplement. Make sure you look for the Creapure trademark because they will assure you that you'll have one hundred percent pure product.

When should I take it? It doesn't matter very much, seeing as it doesn't have an instant effect. Some people like to say that you should take it after your workout. These people like to cite studies that say there is better absorption after a workout, but here's the thing: in those studies, the researchers actually declared that the difference was so tiny that it wasn't statistically relevant. You do you. You take it when you can.

How much? 3-5 grams per day (like a teaspoon). That's enough to saturate the muscle within 2 to 4 weeks. If you take excess, cool, but you'll just pee the excess out, and it won't help.

With what liquid should I mix creatine? Great news—whatever kind of drink you want. Traditionally, it was a juice or very sugary drink, but research has proven this does nothing very beneficial.

Should I have a loading phase? Loading phases are when you take 20 grams per day for 5-7 days before going to the recommended amount of 3-5. Do this if you want, but it won't be all that important. Initially, a higher level will lead to a faster saturation of the muscle cells, but only by a couple days, and the recommended dose will do the same thing anyway.

Should I cycle creatine? Nope! If you decide to stop taking it at any point, your body will be completely fine. You will have no side effects or withdrawal symptoms, other than the decrease in strength.

Vegan Food for Energy

Theoretically, every food has calories, and calories give you energy, so it would make sense that every food would provide you with energy, with very high-calorie foods giving you the most energy. This is not quite right, unfortunately, if you consider longterm effects. Fortunately for us, there are plenty of foods that can help you get energy without compromising you in the long term. Here's what to look for!

Quality carbs. Even though they aren't vital to your survival like some other kinds of foods, they're an excellent energy source, and they're fantastic for instant energy boosts. The more intense that your workouts are, the more important carbs become. Fats provide up to 90 percent of your energy during normal activities, but when you start getting into moderate and high-intensity workouts, it shifts into overdrive and carbs start providing energy. Focus on unprocessed or minimally processed carbs like pasta, whole-grain bread, brown rice, and sweet potatoes. Bonus points for being very nutritious and being high in fiber!

Fruits. They are also carbs, but they get their own section because they hit a lot faster. If you need instant energy, you're not going to find a better source.

Coffee and tea. Well, duh. Tea takes longer to break down than coffee, so it's better for the long term, drawn-out a release of caffeine. Use them before a workout, and it'll increase your performance, but be careful—your body will get used to caffeine levels and you'll have to start drinking more and more over time.

Anything you're deficient in. If you're feeling low on energy, it could be a nutrition deficiency. I'm going to leave you with this: blood tests will tell you if you have a nutritional deficiency. If you live in cold places, you're more likely to be deficient in Vitamin D. Athletes are particularly susceptible to Vitamin C, magnesium, and iron deficiencies (which, fortunately, is an easy fix with a diet adjustment or with the right supplement). Vegan or vegetarian? You might be lacking vitamin B12 and calcium. If this is you, I have good news: these are common problems, and if you get rid of these deficiencies, you should expect a massive energy boost, and your quality of life will increase exponentially as such.

BREAKFAST

Carrots and Raisins Muffins

Ready in Time: 35 minutes | Servings: 4

Ingredients

1 1/4 cup almond flour
1/2 cup whole grain flour (any)
3 Tbsp ground almonds
2 cups carrot, grated
1 1/2 tsp baking soda
2 tsp baking powder
2 tsp cinnamon
1/2 tsp salt
1 tsp apple vinegar
1/2 cup extra-virgin olive oil
2 Tbsp linseed oil
4 Tbsp organic honey
3 oz raisins seedless

Instructions

1. Preheat oven to 360 F.
2. In a big bowl, combine together almond flour, whole grain flour, baking soda, baking powder, cinnamon, and salt.
3. In a separate bowl, whisk apple vinegar, olive oil, linseed oil, and honey.
4. Combine almond flour mixture with liquid mixture; stir well.
5. Add in the shredded carrots and raisins; stir well.
6. Fill the muffin cups 3/4 of the way full.
7. Bake for 30 minutes.
8. Remove from the oven, and allow to cool for 10 minutes.
9. Serve.

Nutrition Facts

Percent daily values based on the Reference Daily Intake (RDI) for a 2000 calorie diet.

Amount Per Serving

Calories 352.31 | Calories From Fat (28%) 100.15 | Total Fat 11.51g 18% | Saturated Fat 1.4g 7% | Cholesterol 0mg 0% | Sodium 813.86mg 34% | Potassium 736.68mg 21% | Total Carbohydrates 62.35g 21% | Fiber 5g 20% | Sugar 33.82g | Protein 7.42g 11%

Green Protein Tornado Smoothie

Ready in Time: 10 minutes | Servings:2

Ingredients

1 avocado (diced)
1 cup fresh spinach (chopped)
1 cup fresh peppermint leaves, chopped
1 banana frozen or fresh
1 cup coconut milk canned
1/2 cup shredded coconut
1/2 cup ground nuts (almonds, peanuts)
1 scoop vegan pea protein powder
2 Tbsp extracted honey (or to taste)
Ice cubes

Instructions

1. Place all ingredients in your high-speed blender and blend until smooth.
2. Serve in chilled glasses with ice cubes.

Nutrition Facts

Percent daily values based on the Reference Daily Intake (RDI) for a 2000 calorie diet.

Amount per Serving

Calories 805.81 | Calories From Fat (67%) 542.27 | Total Fat 64.73g 100% | Saturated Fat 32.11g 161% Cholesterol 1.16mg <1% | Sodium 64.66mg 3% | Potassium 1450mg 41% | Total Carbohydrates 53.5g 18% | Fiber 14.19g 57% | Sugar 28.2g | Protein 18.14g 36%

Multi Protein Smoothie

Ready in Time: 10 minutes | Servings:2

Ingredients

2 cups of soy milk
1 scoop soy protein powder
4 Tbsp Steel-cut oatmeal
4 Tbsp grated nuts
2 cups fresh spinach, coarsely chopped
1 ripe banana, fresh or frozen
1/2 tsp ground cinnamon
1/2 tsp ground nutmeg
1/2 tsp ground cloves
3 Tbsp Maple syrup or honey
1 tsp pure vanilla extract
2 Tbsp chia seeds for serving

Instructions

1. Combine all the ingredients in your fast-speed blender.
2. Run the blender until all ingredients are thoroughly blended and smooth.
3. Sprinkle with chia seeds and serve.

Nutrition Facts

Percent daily values based on the Reference Daily Intake (RDI) for a 2000 calorie diet.

Amount Per Serving

Calories 409.84 | Calories From Fat (32%) 131.8 | Total Fat 15.33g 24% | Saturated Fat 1.7g 8% | Cholesterol 1.16mg <1% | Sodium 187.28mg 8% | Potassium 846,4mg 24% | Total Carbohydrates 55g 18% | Fiber 6.36g 25% | Sugar 35.36g | Protein 16.4g 32%

Nutty Silken Tofu with Berries Smoothie

Ready in Time: 10 minutes | Servings:2

Ingredients

1 cup of soy milk

1/2 cup of silken tofu

1 Tbsp almond butter (unsweetened)

1 frozen banana sliced

2 Tbsp Steel-cut oatmeal

2 Tbsp ground almonds

2 Tbsp ground cashews

1 tsp pure vanilla extract

1 cup fresh or frozen berries (blueberries, raspberries, blackberries, and strawberries)

2 Tbsp agave or maple syrup

Instructions

1. Add all ingredients in your high-speed blender.
2. Blend until smooth.
3. Serve and enjoy your liquid breakfast.

Nutrition Facts

Percent daily values based on the Reference Daily Intake (RDI) for a 2000 calorie diet.

Amount Per Serving

Calories 534.45 | Calories From Fat (32%) 173.5 | Total Fat 20.38g 31% | Saturated Fat 2.49g 12% | Cholesterol 0mg 0% | Sodium 122mg 5% | Potassium 744.56mg 21% | Total Carbohydrates 76.7g 26% | Fiber 6.78g 27% | Sugar 35.7g | Protein 17.6g 32%

Oat - Raspberries Granola

Ready in Time: 35 minutes | Servings: 5

Ingredients

2 cups oats
1/2 cup oat bran
2 Tbsp flaxseed meal
2/3 cup almonds, chopped
1/2 cup shredded coconut
1/2 cup dried cranberries, chopped
1 tsp cinnamon
1/4 tsp salt
3 Tbsp sesame oil
4 Tbsp maple syrup or honey
1 cup raspberries row or frozen

Instructions

1. Preheat the oven to 325 F/160 C.
2. Stir together the oats, oat bran, flax, almonds, coconut, dried fruit, cinnamon, and salt.
3. In a bowl, stir together sesame oil and maple syrup and microwave for about 30 seconds.
4. Stir and then microwave for a further 30 seconds.
5. Pour the hot mixture over the dry and stir to combine well.
6. Spread a mixture evenly into a baking tray.
7. Sprinkle fresh raspberries evenly over the mixture
8. Bake for 18-20 minutes.
9. Serve hot or cold with vegetable milk, honey, fruits, etc.
10. Store cold granola an airtight container, in a cool, dry spot for six months (sometimes longer).

Nutrition Facts

Percent daily values based on the Reference Daily Intake (RDI) for a 2000 calorie diet.

Amount Per Serving

Calories 590.72 | Calories From Fat (34%) 199.78 | Total Fat 23.85g 37% | Saturated Fat 4.38g 22% | Cholesterol 0mg 0% | Sodium 212.23mg 9% | Potassium 704mg 20% | Total Carbohydrates 81.68g 27% | Fiber 14.2g 60% | Sugar 17.48g | Protein 19g 38%

Porridge with Oatmeal and Maca Powder

Ready in Time: 15 minutes | Servings: 2

Ingredients

2 cups almond milk (or coconut milk) unsweetened

1 pinch of table salt

1 cup rolled oats

1 1/2 Tbsp Maca powder

1 Tbsp honey (or maple syrup)

1 tsp ground cinnamon

1 banana peeled and thinly sliced

Instructions

1. In a saucepan, heat almond milk with a pinch of salt over high heat; bring to boiling.

2. Stir in rolled oats and Maca powder, reduce heat to medium and simmer, uncovered, for 5 to 7 minutes; stir constantly.

3. Place oatmeal in a bowl and pour over the honey, cinnamon, and banana slices.

4. Serve and enjoy!

Nutrition Facts

Percent daily values based on the Reference Daily Intake (RDI) for a 2000 calorie diet.

Amount Per Serving

Calories 481.64 | Calories From Fat (19%) 91.71 | Total Fat 9.68g 15% | Saturated Fat 0.52g 3% | Cholesterol 0mg 0% | Sodium 437.9mg 18% | Potassium 1368mg 39% | Total Carbohydrates 90.59g 30% | Fiber 9.8g 40% | Sugar 32.32g | Protein 16g 32%

Savory Potato-Turmeric Pancakes

Ready in Time: 20 minutes | Servings: 4

Ingredients

4 large potatoes, grated
1 tsp of turmeric powder
1 Tbsp almond butter with salt added
Salt and ground pepper to taste
1/2 cup of garlic-infused olive oil
Serving: fresh chopped parsley or sliced green onions

Instructions

1. Peel, wash, and pat dry potatoes.
2. Grate potatoes over a plate or bowl.
3. Season potatoes with the salt and pepper and turmeric.
4. Heat oil in a large frying skillet over medium-strong heat
5. Spoon grated potatoes into hot oil and press with a spatula.
6. Cook for about 2 minutes; flip the pancake and cook until golden brown.
7. Transfer pancake to the kitchen paper towel.
8. Serve warm with chopped parsley or green onion.

Nutrition Facts

Percent daily values based on the Reference Daily Intake (RDI) for a 2000 calorie diet.

Amount Per Serving

Calories 406.87 | Calories From Fat (64%) 259.11 | Total Fat 29.44g 45% | Saturated Fat 4g 20% | Cholesterol 0mg 0% | Sodium 165.73mg 7% | Potassium 818.75mg 23% | Total Carbohydrates 33.25g 11% | Fiber 4.58g 18% | Sugar 1.63g | Protein 6g 12%

Sheer Vegan Meatza

Ready in Time: 1 hour and 5 minutes | Servings: 3

Ingredients

Cauliflower Crust

1/2 cup avocado oil

1 head cauliflower cut into florets

1/2 tsp garlic minced

Salt and ground pepper to taste

1/2 cup button mushrooms thinly sliced

2 Tbsp arrowroot powder

Filling/topping

1/2 cup of ketchup

1 cup mushrooms sliced

1 cup avocado puree (mashed)

1/2 cup grated carrot

1 cup olives, pitted, sliced or halved

Instructions

Cauliflower dough:

1. Preheat oven to 400F.
2. Cover a baking sheet with parchment paper.
3. Add cauliflower florets into your food processor into batches.
4. Process cauliflower florets until they achieve a form of rice.
5. Cook cauliflower in non-stick frying skillet for about 8 to 10 minutes.
6. Transfer cauliflower rice into a bowl and add mushrooms, ground garlic, arrowroot powder, some oil, and the salt and pepper; stir well.
7. Spread cauliflower dough onto a prepared baking sheet, and bake for about 20 minutes.
8. Remove from oven, and allow it to cool for 10 minutes.

Toppings

1. Fill the dough with ketchup, avocado puree, sliced mushrooms, carrot, and sprinkle with little avocado oil.
2. Place dough in the oven and bake for 10 to 12 minutes.
3. Slice and serve hot.

Nutrition Facts

Percent daily values based on the Reference Daily Intake (RDI) for a 2000 calorie diet.

Amount Per Serving

Calories 391 | Calories From Fat (64%) 248.82 | Total Fat 28.62g 44% | Saturated Fat 3.59g 18% | Cholesterol 0mg 0% | Sodium 911.7mg 38% | Potassium 1117.1mg 32% | Total Carbohydrates 33.57g 11% | Fiber 8.8g 36% | Sugar 14.9g | Protein 8g 16%

Sour Edamame Spread

Ready in Time: 10 minutes | Servings: 6

Ingredients

2 cups frozen unshelled edamame, cooked according to package directions

1/4 cup sesame oil

1 cup silken tofu, drained

1 Tbsp minced garlic (from 3 medium cloves)

Flaky sea salt to taste

White pepper to taste

2 tsp ground cumin

1 Tbsp rice vinegar

4 Tbsp fresh lemon juice

Sesame seeds for serving

Instructions

1. Place all ingredients into your high-speed blender or into a food processor.
2. Blend until combined well.
3. Transfer spread to a bowl and a sprinkle with sesame seeds.
4. Edamame spread can be refrigerated in an airtight container up to 3 days.

Nutrition Facts

Percent daily values based on the Reference Daily Intake (RDI) for a 2000 calorie diet.

Amount Per Serving

Calories 235.56 | Calories From Fat (50%) 118.59 | Total Fat 13.3g 21% | Saturated Fat 1.85g 9% | Cholesterol 0mg 0% | Sodium 35.82mg 1% | Potassium 298.47mg 9% | Total Carbohydrates 21.2g 7% Fiber 3.06g 12% | Sugar 2.89g | Protein 9g 18%

Spicy Banana, Oat & Coconut Mash

Ready in Time: 30 minutes | Servings: 4

Ingredients

3 bananas, peeled and sliced
2 cup coconut milk canned
2 cup of water
1/2 cup Steel-cut oatmeal
1/2 cup of coconut sugar
1 tsp of pure vanilla extract
1/4 tsp of ground nutmeg
1/4 tsp of ground cinnamon
Serving: banana slices and honey

Instructions

1. Add banana and coconut milk into your high-speed blender; blend until combined well.
2. Boil water in a saucepan on medium-high heat.
3. Pour in the banana mixture, and steel-cut oatmeal and cook, while whisking constantly, for 4 to 5 minutes.
4. Reduce heat to low, cover, and let simmer for 10 minutes.
5. Add coconut sugar, vanilla extract, cinnamon, and nutmeg.
6. Stir for a further two minutes and remove from heat.
7. Serve hot with banana slices and honey.

Nutrition Facts

Percent daily values based on the Reference Daily Intake (RDI) for a 2000 calorie diet.

Amount Per Serving

Calories 495.54 | Calories From Fat (45%) 222.6 | Total Fat 26.54g 41% | Saturated Fat 21.75g 109% Cholesterol 0mg 0% | Sodium 71.15mg 3% | Potassium 699.3mg 20% | Total Carbohydrates 66.92g 22% | Fiber 4.64g 19% | Sugar 34.22g | Protein 7g 14%

Stamina Tofu "Omelette"

Ready in Time: 20 minutes | Servings: 2

Ingredients

2 Tbsp of olive oil
1 small onion finely chopped
1 large red pepper chopped
1/2 cup white mushrooms halved or sliced
3/4 lb tofu cut into cubes
1 Tbsp nutritional yeast
1 tsp turmeric (for color)
1 tsp of garlic powder
Sea salt and ground black pepper to taste

Instructions

1. Heat oil in a large frying pan over medium-high heat.
2. Sauté onion and red pepper with a pinch of salt for 2 to 3 minutes.
3. Add mushrooms and cook until most of the water from the mushrooms has evaporated.
4. Add tofu cubes and all remaining ingredients; stir well.
5. Cover and cook over medium heat for about 6 to 8 minutes; stir occasionally.
6. Taste and adjust seasonings.
7. Serve hot.

Nutrition Facts

Percent daily values based on the Reference Daily Intake (RDI) for a 2000 calorie diet.

Amount Per Serving

Calories 350.37 | Calories From Fat (60%) 209.61 | Total Fat 24.29g 37% | Saturated Fat 2.92g 15% | Cholesterol 0mg 0% | Sodium 24.16mg 1% | Potassium 623.77mg 18% | Total Carbohydrates 17.6g 6% | Fiber 5.28g 21% | Sugar 7g | Protein 21.6g 43%

Superelan Vegan Quark Smoothie

Ready in Time: 10 minutes | Servings: 2

Ingredients

1 frozen banana

3/4 cup frozen berries

1 apple cored and sliced

1/3 cup oats

1 scoop vegan protein powder (Soy or Hemp Protein)

3/4 cup vegan quark (for example Alpro)

1 1/2 cups almond milk

Instructions

1. Place all ingredients into your fast-speed blender.
2. Blend until smooth and creamy.
3. Serve immediately.

Nutrition Facts

Percent daily values based on the Reference Daily Intake (RDI) for a 2000 calorie diet.

Amount Per Serving

Calories 439.31 | Calories From Fat (27%) 116.9 | Total Fat 13.39g 21% | Saturated Fat 6g 30% | Cholesterol 33mg 11% | Sodium 114.18mg 5% | Potassium 553.73mg 16% | Total Carbohydrates 76.31g 25% | Fiber 12.2g 49% | Sugar 38.69g | Protein 12g 24%

Sweet Potato and Orange Breakfast Bread

Ready in Time: 55 minutes | Servings: 6

Ingredients

1 large sweet potato (about 12 oz.), peeled and shredded
1/2 cup fresh orange juice
1/3 cup water
1/3 cup orange marmalade
4 Tbsp canola oil
1 Tbsp arrowroot powder
3 cups flour self-rising
1/2 cup sugar
2 tsp baking powder
1/4 tsp salt

Instructions

1. Preheat oven to 375 F/180 C.
2. In a small saucepan, cook the shredded sweet potato for 10 min; drain and cool.
3. In a bowl, combine shredder potato with orange juice, water, orange marmalade, canola oil, and arrowroot powder.
4. In a separate bowl, combine together the flour, sugar, baking powder, and salt.
5. Add the liquid ingredients to the flour mixture and stir just until combined.
6. Spoon batter into greased loaf pan and bake for 30-35 minutes.
7. When ready, allow it to cool for 10 minutes.
8. Slice and serve.

Nutrition Facts

Percent daily values based on the Reference Daily Intake (RDI) for a 2000 calorie diet.

Amount Per Serving

Calories 481.94 | Calories From Fat (18%) 88.1 | Total Fat 10g 15% | Saturated Fat 0.9g 4% | Cholesterol 0mg 0% | Sodium 273.26mg 11% | Potassium 374.4mg 11% | Total Carbohydrates 91.61g 31% | Fiber 2.38g 10% | Sugar 36.31g | Protein 7.58g 15%

The Power of Banana & Soya Smoothie

Ready in Time: 10 minutes | Servings: 2

Ingredients

3/4 cup soya milk

2 bananas frozen

1 kiwi fruit sliced

1 Tbsp hemp seeds

1 Tbsp linseed oil

1 scoop vegan protein powder (pea or soy protein)

1 cup fresh spinach

3/4 cup frozen berries thawed (unsweetened)

Instructions

1. Place all ingredients in your blender.
2. Blend for about 45 seconds or until everything is well mixed.
3. Serve.

Nutrition Facts

Percent daily values based on the Reference Daily Intake (RDI) for a 2000 calorie diet.

Amount Per Serving

Calories 325.59 | Calories From Fat (38%) 122.54 | Total Fat 13.57g 21% | Saturated Fat 1.61g 8% | Cholesterol 2.31mg <1% | Sodium 157.75mg 7% | Potassium 916mg 26% | Total Carbohydrates 45.5g 15% | Fiber 7.82g 31% | Sugar 23g | Protein 10g 20%

Toasted Tempeh - Vegan Mayo Sandwich

Ready in Time: 10 minutes | Servings: 1

Ingredients

2 slices of bread
2 Tbsp of Vegan Mayo
2 slices of smoky Tempeh cut into strips
1 large tomato sliced
4 leaves of lettuce

Instructions

1. Toast your bread and then spread a layer of Vegan Mayo on one side of each slice of bread.
2. Layer the Tempeh onto one side of bread and top with tomato slices and lettuce leaves.
3. Cover with the second slice of bread.
4. Enjoy!

Nutrition Facts

Percent daily values based on the Reference Daily Intake (RDI) for a 2000 calorie diet.

Amount Per Serving

Calories 535.27 | Calories From Fat (29%) 156.34 | Total Fat 18.69g 29% | Saturated Fat 2.7g 14% | Cholesterol 0mg 0% | Sodium 186.34mg 8% | Potassium 913.45mg 26% | Total Carbohydrates 59.41g 20% | Fiber 8.12g 32% | Sugar 3.73g | Protein 39.86g 80%

Vegan Parsley and Almond Bread

Preparation Time: 1 hour | Inactive Time: 10 minutes | Servings: 4

Ingredients

1 1/2 cups sparkling water on room temperature
1 Tbsp of active dry yeast
1 tsp sugar
3 Tbsp olive oil
2 1/2 cups self-rising flour
2 Tbsp fresh minced parsley
1/2 cup almonds finely chopped
1 tsp ground garlic
1 tsp salt

Instructions

1. Preheat oven to 375 F/185 C.
2. Grease a baking loaf with olive oil; set aside.
3. In a large bowl, dissolve yeast, sugar, and salt in sparkling water; let stand until bubbles form on the surface.
4. Add in flour and olive oil and beat until smooth.
5. Add all remaining ingredients, and continue to beat until combined well or until form soft dough.
6. Turn onto a floured surface; knead until smooth and elastic or for about 8 minutes.
7. Shape dough into a loaf, and place into a prepared bread loaf.
8. Bake for 30 to 35 minutes or until golden brown.
9. Remove from oven, and let sit for 10 minutes.
10. Slice, serve, and enjoy!

Nutrition Facts

Percent daily values based on the Reference Daily Intake (RDI) for a 2000 calorie diet.

Amount Per Serving

Calories 485.56 | Calories From Fat (35%) 171.85 | Total Fat 19g 31% | Saturated Fat 2.23g 11% | Cholesterol 0mg 0% | Sodium 604mg 25% | Potassium 231.32mg 7% | Total Carbohydrates 65g 22% Fiber 4.34g 17% | Sugar 2.13g | Protein 12.56g 25%

Vegan Sloppy Joe with Tofu

Ready in Time: 25 minutes | Servings: 4

Ingredients

2 Tbsp avocado oil
1 onion finely sliced
2 cloves garlic finely sliced
1 lb tofu cheese, cubed
1 jalapeno pepper sliced
1 green bell pepper, diced
1 large tomato diced
3 Tbsp tomato paste
2 Tbsp fajita spice mix
Salt and ground black pepper
1 cup of water

Instructions

1. Heat oil in large frying skillet over medium heat.
2. Add sliced green onion, garlic, green pepper, and jalapeno pepper; sauté with a pinch of pepper for 3 to 4 minutes or until soft.
3. Add tofu and brown for a further 3 minutes; stir constantly.
4. Add diced tomato, tomato paste, water, and fajita spice mix; cover and cook on medium-low heat for 10 minutes.
5. Taste and adjust salt and pepper to taste.
6. Serve immediately or keep refrigerated.

Nutrition Facts

Percent daily values based on the Reference Daily Intake (RDI) for a 2000 calorie diet.

Amount Per Serving

Calories 217.15 | Calories From Fat (55%) 119.7 | Total Fat 13.93g 21% | Saturated Fat 1.49g 7% | Cholesterol 0mg 0% | Sodium 271.82mg 11% | Potassium 610.52mg 17% | Total Carbohydrates 14.39g 5% | Fiber 3.36g 13% | Sugar 7.09g | Protein 13.41g 27%

Vegan Super Green Giant Smoothie

Ready in Time: 10 minutes | Servings: 2

Ingredients

1 1/2 cups almond milk (or coconut milk)
1 cup of carrot tops chopped
1 cup fresh spinach chopped
1 cucumber, peeled and sliced
1 large banana, fresh or frozen
3 Tbsp ground almonds or ground Macadamia almonds
1 scoop vegan protein powder (pea or soy protein)
1 Tbsp extracted honey
1 Tbsp linseed oil

Instructions

1. Place all ingredients in your fast-speed blender.
2. Blend until smooth and combined well.
3. Serve.

Nutrition Facts

Percent daily values based on the Reference Daily Intake (RDI) for a 2000 calorie diet.

Amount Per Serving

Calories 252.71 | Calories From Fat (46%) 117.03 | Total Fat 12.74g 20% | Saturated Fat 0.74g 4% | Cholesterol 2.31mg <1% | Sodium 262.17mg 11% | Potassium 588mg 17% | Total Carbohydrates 24.2g 8% | Fiber 4.15g 17% | Sugar 14.57g | Protein 10.85g 22%

Vegan Sweet "French Toast"

Ready in Time: 15 minutes | Servings: 2

Ingredients

3 Tbsp olive oil
1 cup of soy milk (unsweetened)
1 cup oat flour (or buckwheat)
1/2 tsp cinnamon
2 Tbsp brown sugar or sugar
6 slices day-old bread (or multi-grain bread)
Servings; vegan spread, groundnuts, honey or Maple syrup

Instructions

1. Heat oil in a frying skillet over medium-high heat.
2. Pour soy milk in one bowl.
3. In a separate bowl, combine together oat flakes and brown sugar; stir well.
4. Dip each bread slice first in soy milk, and then roll into oat flakes mixture.
5. Fry your vegan French toast for a couple of minutes on each side, or until golden brown.
6. Remove French toast onto a lined plate with kitchen paper to drain.
7. Serve with your favorite vegan spread, groundnuts, honey or Maple syrup.

Nutrition Facts

Percent daily values based on the Reference Daily Intake (RDI) for a 2000 calorie diet.

Amount Per Serving

Calories 482.22 | Calories From Fat (29%) 139.4 | Total Fat 15.79g 24% | Saturated Fat 2.92g 15% | Cholesterol 0mg 0% | Sodium 185.87mg 8% | Potassium 564.6mg 16% | Total Carbohydrates 76.75g 26% | Fiber 8.03g 32% | Sugar 25.06g | Protein 13g 26%

Vigorous Dragon Fruit Smoothie

Ready in Time: 15 minutes | Servings: 2

Ingredients

1 Dragon fruit (red) about 3/4 lb
1 large ripe banana
1 cup of coconut milk
1/2 cup of shredded coconut
3 Tbsp ground nuts
1 cup of baby spinach fresh
1 scoop vegan protein powder (soy or pea)
1 glass of crushed ice cubes

Instructions

1. Cut the dragon fruit in half.
2. With the help of a sharp knife slice right through it, scoop out the flesh with a spoon.
3. Place dragon fruit flesh in your blender along with all remaining ingredients.
4. Blend it until completely smooth.
5. Serve immediately.

Nutrition Facts

Percent daily values based on the Reference Daily Intake (RDI) for a 2000 calorie diet.

Amount Per Serving

Calories 841.54 | Calories From Fat (83%) 742.54 | Total Fat 87g 134% | Saturated Fat 69.33g 347% | Cholesterol 1.16mg <1% | Sodium 48.19mg 2% | Potassium 969.49mg 28% | Total Carbohydrates 33.19g 11% | Fiber 5.38g 22% | Sugar 17.7g | Protein 9.8g 20%

LUNCH

Asian Chilled Cucumber and Seaweed Soup

Ready in Time: 15 minutes | Servings: 6

Ingredients

1 cup soaked seaweed, rinsed * see note
2 cucumbers cut into thin slices
Seasonings
4 Tbsp of soy sauce
1/4 cup fresh lemon juice
1/2 tsp garlic minced
1 Tbsp red pepper flakes
2 tsp sesame seeds toasted
1 tsp brown sugar
4 cups of water
Sea salt to taste

Instructions

1. Soak seaweed in water to cover overnight.
2. When soft, drain and cut into 2-inch pieces.
3. Boil water with a little salt in a pot.
4. Blanch drained seaweed for 20 to 25 seconds; plunge into the ice water.
5. In a bowl, combine together cucumber, seaweed, and all remaining ingredients; stir well.
6. Refrigerate to chill well.
7. Taste and adjust salt to taste.
8. Serve in chilled bowls.

Nutrition Facts

Percent daily values based on the Reference Daily Intake (RDI) for a 2000 calorie diet.

Amount Per Serving

Calories 49.06 | Calories From Fat (15%) 7.18 | Total Fat 0.86g 1% | Saturated Fat 0.2g 1% | Cholesterol 0mg 0% | Sodium 440.87mg 18% | Potassium 238,19mg 7% | Total Carbohydrates 10.11g 3% | Fiber 1.29g 5% | Sugar 3.41g | Protein 3g 6%

Note: Because of its increasing popularity, many major supermarket chains carry dried seaweed in their Asian foods aisle.

Baked "Hasselback" Sweet Potatoes

Ready in Time: 1 hour and 15 minutes | Servings: 4

Ingredients

1/2 cup olive oil
1 Tbsp of fresh rosemary finely chopped
4 large sweet potatoes, chopped
1/2 tsp ground mustard
Kosher salt and freshly ground black pepper
1 cup Tofu grated (optional)

Instructions

1. Preheat oven to 425 F.
2. Wash and rub potatoes; cut trough potatoes about halfway into thin slices (as Hasselback potatoes).
3. Combine olive, rosemary, and ground mustard; generously brush potatoes.
4. Place sweet potatoes on a greased baking sheet.
5. Bake for 60 minutes or until soft.
6. Remove from the oven, and let cool for 10 minutes.
7. Serve with grated Tofu (optional).

Nutrition Facts

Percent daily values based on the Reference Daily Intake (RDI) for a 2000 calorie diet.

Amount Per Serving

Calories 285.21 | Calories From Fat (92%) 263.44 | Total Fat 30g 46% | Saturated Fat 4g 20% | Cholesterol 0mg 0% | Sodium 12.48mg <1% | Potassium 69.92mg 2% | Total Carbohydrates 1.13g <1% | Sugar 0.25g | Protein 5g 10%

Baked Buffalo Cauliflower 'Wings'

Ready in Time: 30 minutes | Servings: 4

Ingredients

2 Tbsp olive oil
1 cup of soy milk
1 cup soy flour
2 tsp garlic powder
1 head of cauliflower, chopped into flowerets
1 cup Red Hot Sauce (or vegan Buffalo sauce)
2 Tbsp of avocado oil

Instructions

1. Preheat the oven to 450 F/225 C.
2. Grease a shallow baking dish with olive oil; set aside.
3. In a bowl, stir together soy milk, soy flour, and garlic powder until well combined.
4. Coat the cauliflower florets with the soy flour mixture and place in a prepared baking dish.
5. Bake for 18 to 20 minutes.
6. In a meanwhile, heat Red Hot Sauce or vegan Buffalo sauce with avocado oil in a saucepan.
7. Pour the hot sauce over the baked cauliflower and bake for an additional 6 to 8 minutes.
8. Serve hot.

Nutrition Facts

Percent daily values based on the Reference Daily Intake (RDI) for a 2000 calorie diet.

Amount Per Serving

Calories 360.35 | Calories From Fat (63%) 225.7 | Total Fat 25.93g 40% | Saturated Fat 3.54g 18% | Cholesterol 0mg 0% | Sodium 953.78mg 40% | Potassium 1286.29mg 37% | Total Carbohydrates 23.49g 8% | Fiber 7.32g 29% | Sugar 8g | Protein 14g 28%

Baked Creamy Corn with Shredded Tofu

Ready in Time: 25 minutes | Servings: 4

Ingredients

4 Tbsp rice oil

3 cups sweet corn kernels (frozen or fresh)

2 green onions, thinly sliced

1 cup vegan mayonnaise

1 Tbsp brown sugar

Salt and pepper to taste

8 oz silken tofu shredded

Instructions

1. Preheat oven to 400 F/200 C.
2. Grease a baking dish with rice oil.
3. In a bowl, combine together corn kernels, green onions. Vegan mayonnaise, brown sugar, and salt and pepper; stir to combine well.
4. Pour the corn mixture into a prepared baking dish.
5. Sprinkle evenly with shredded tofu.
6. Bake for 14 to 16 minutes.
7. Remove from the oven and allow it to cool.
8. Serve.

Nutrition Facts

Percent daily values based on the Reference Daily Intake (RDI) for a 2000 calorie diet.

Amount Per Serving

Calories 482 | Calories From Fat (65%) 312.49 | Total Fat 35.37g 54% | Saturated Fat 5.86g 29% | Cholesterol 15.28mg 5% | Sodium 425.49mg 18% | Potassium 338.68mg 10% | Total Carbohydrates 40.56g 14% | Fiber 2.4g 10% | Sugar 10.48g | Protein 7.16g 14%

Baked Tamari-Tofu and Cabbage Salad

Ready in Time: 45 minutes | Servings: 4

Ingredients

1 lb firm tofu, drained and cut into 1/2-inch slabs
1/2 cup tamari sauce
1 lb shredded cabbage
2 shredded carrots
1 onion finely sliced
Sea salt and ground pepper to taste
4 Tbsp sesame oil
1 Tbsp fresh ginger grated
1 tsp hot chili paste
3 Tbsp rice vinegar or apple cider vinegar
2 cloves garlic minced
4 Tbsp water

Instructions

1. Preheat the oven to 375 degrees F.
2. Grease a baking sheet with some oil and set aside.
3. Toss Tofu slabs with 1/4 cup of the tamari sauce.
4. Arrange the tofu on the prepared baking sheet and bake for 25 to 30 minutes.
5. Remove from the oven and set aside to cool.
6. In a large bowl, combine the cabbage, carrots, and onion; season with the salt and pepper, and set aside.
7. In a separate bowl, combine sesame oil, ginger, chili paste, and remaining 1/4 cup of tamari sauce, vinegar, garlic, and water.
8. Pour the garlic-ginger mixture over the cabbage mixture and toss to combine.
9. Taste and adjust seasonings.
10. Serve topped with tofu.

Nutrition Facts

Percent daily values based on the Reference Daily Intake (RDI) for a 2000 calorie diet.

Amount Per Serving

Calories 386 | Calories From Fat (55%) 213.87 | Total Fat 24.8g 38% | Saturated Fat 3.58g 18% | Cholesterol 0mg 0% | Sodium 2080mg 87% | Potassium 759.94mg 22% | Total Carbohydrates 21.52g 7% | Fiber 7.1g 31% | Sugar 7.54g | Protein 25.8g 52%

High-Protein Minestrone Soup (Crock Pot)

Ready in Time: 8 hours | Servings: 6

Ingredients

1 cup dried beans, soaked
1 onion finely chopped
2 cloves garlic finely chopped
1 large carrot peeled and cut into 1/2-inch slices
1 cup shredded cabbage
1 stalk celery cut into 1-inch chunks
1 cup fresh chard chopped
1 zucchini sliced
1 large potato peeled and diced
1 cup tomato paste
2 cups vegetable broth
1/2 cup olive oil
Salt and ground pepper to taste

Instructions

1. Soak beans overnight.
2. Place all ingredients into your 6 quarts Crock-Pot.
3. Give a good stir and cover.
4. Cook on HIGH for 4 to 5 hours or on LOW heat for 8 hours.
5. Taste, and adjust salt and pepper.
6. Serve hot.

Nutrition Facts

Percent daily values based on the Reference Daily Intake (RDI) for a 2000 calorie diet.

Amount Per Serving

Calories 263.29 | Calories From Fat (6%) 16.82 | Total Fat 2g 3% | Saturated Fat 0.45g 2% | Cholesterol 0.2mg <1% | Sodium 751.11mg 31% | Potassium 1435.7mg 41% | Total Carbohydrates 50.7g 17% | Fiber 10.12g 40% | Sugar 5.39g | Protein 13.19g 26%

Hot Sour and Spicy Bok Choy Salad

Ready in Time: 20 minutes | Servings: 4

Ingredients

1/3 cup sesame oil
1 onion finely chopped
2 cloves garlic, minced
Salt and ground pepper to taste
1 1/2 lbs Bok Choy (chopped)
2 Tbsp of lime juice
1 tsp crushed red pepper
1/2 tsp hot chili pepper finely chopped
1 tsp garlic powder
1/2 cup water

Instructions

1. Trim the Bok Choy stems off and rinse under cold water; place into a colander to drain.
2. Heat oil in a large frying skillet over medium heat.
3. Sauté onion and garlic with a pinch of salt until soft or for 3 to 4 minutes.
4. Add Bok Choy and slightly stir.
5. Cover and cook for about 3 to 4 minutes.
6. Add fresh lime juice, crushed pepper, chili pepper, and garlic powder.
7. Pour water and simmer for a further 4 to 5 minutes.
8. Taste and adjust salt and pepper to taste.
9. Serve hot.

Nutrition Facts

Percent daily values based on the Reference Daily Intake (RDI) for a 2000 calorie diet.

Amount Per Serving

Calories 183.95 | Calories From Fat (88%) 161 | Total Fat 18.22g 28% | Saturated Fat 2.6g 13% | Cholesterol 0mg 0% | Sodium 342.5mg 14% | Potassium 92.71mg 3% | Total Carbohydrates 5g 2% Fiber 0.77g 3% | Sugar 1.6g | Protein 2g 4%

Integral Rotini Pasta with Vegetables

Ready in Time: 35 minutes | Servings: 4

Ingredients

1 lb whole-grain pasta rotini
4 Tbsp olive oil
2 cups zucchini - cut into small cubes
1 red onion, cut into cubes
1 red bell pepper sliced
1 cup of vegetable broth
1 cup cherry tomatoes halved
2 cloves garlic finely sliced
1/2 cup fresh basil finely chopped
2 Tbsp lemon juice (freshly squeezed)
Salt and ground pepper to taste

Instructions

1. Cook rotini pasta according to the instructions on the package.
2. Rinse and drain into a colander; set aside.
3. Heat oil in a wok or deep frying pan over medium heat.
4. Add zucchini, onion, and red peppers; sauté for about 6 to 7 minutes.
5. Add sliced garlic, a pinch of salt, and stir for 2 minutes.
6. Add cherry tomatoes and vegetable broth; cook for a further 3 to 4 minutes.
7. Add rotini pasta and fresh basil; toss to combine well.
8. Taste and adjust salt and pepper to taste.
9. Serve with lemon juice.

Nutrition Facts

Percent daily values based on the Reference Daily Intake (RDI) for a 2000 calorie diet.

Amount Per Serving

Calories 348.77 | Calories From Fat (50%) 174.3 | Total Fat 19.81g 30% | Saturated Fat 3.81g 19% | Cholesterol 0mg 0% | Sodium 103.66mg 4% | Potassium 690.39mg 20% | Total Carbohydrates 37.38g 12% | Fiber 6.07g 24% | Sugar 3.51g | Protein 9g 18%

Mushrooms and Chickpeas Risotto

Ready in Time: 30 minutes | Servings: 4

Ingredients

1/2 cup olive oil
1 onion finely diced
1 1/2 cups rice basmati
2 cups fresh mushrooms sliced
2 cups vegetable broth
2 cups of water
1/2 lb canned chickpeas, drained and rinsed
1/4 tsp turmeric ground
Salt and pepper to taste

Instructions

1. Heat oil in a deep skillet over medium-high heat.
2. Sauté the onion and rice for 2-3 minutes; stir frequently.
3. Pour the broth, water, sliced mushrooms, turmeric, and boiled chickpeas; stir well.
4. Bring to boil, reduce heat to medium, cover and cook for 18 minutes; stir occasionally.
5. Remove from the heat and let it cool for 5 minutes.
6. Taste and adjust salt and pepper to taste; stir.
7. Serve.

Nutrition Facts

Percent daily values based on the Reference Daily Intake (RDI) for a 2000 calorie diet.

Amount Per Serving

Calories 630.4 | Calories From Fat (41%) 257.56 | Total Fat 29.19g 45% | Saturated Fat 4.17g 21% | Cholesterol 0.62mg <1% | Sodium 582.12mg 24% | Potassium 417.22mg 12% | Total Carbohydrates 81.5g 27% | Fiber 4.19g 17% | Sugar 1.9g | Protein 11g 22%

Pasta Salad with Marinated Artichoke Hearts and Tofu

Ready in Time: 20 minutes | Servings: 4

Ingredients

1 lb medium pasta shape, uncooked
1 can (15 oz) marinated artichoke hearts, drained, chopped
1 cup Tofu firm cut into small cubes
1 cup fresh mushrooms, sliced
1/2 cup onion finely diced
1/3 cup chopped fresh basil
Salt and freshly ground black pepper to taste
2/3 cup vegan salad dressing

Instructions

1. Prepare pasta according to package directions.
2. In a large salad bowl, combine artichoke hearts, Tofu, mushrooms, onion, basil, and the salt and pepper.
3. Rinse pasta with cold water, and drain well.
4. Add pasta and vegan dressing to a salad bowl; toss well.
5. Taste and adjust salt and pepper to taste.
6. Serve or keep refrigerated.

Nutrition Facts

Percent daily values based on the Reference Daily Intake (RDI) for a 2000 calorie diet.

Amount Per Serving

Calories 587.57 | Calories From Fat (15%) 90.63 | Total Fat 10.39g 16% | Saturated Fat 1.59g 8% | Cholesterol 0mg 0% | Sodium 405mg 17% | Potassium 557mg 16% | Total Carbohydrates 101.69g 34% | Fiber 10.91g 44% | Sugar 3.78g | Protein 22.28g 45%

Raw Creamy Coconut - Curry Soup

Ready in Time: 10 minutes | Servings: 2

Ingredients

4 Tbsp sesame oil

1/4 cup coconut aminos or soy sauce

1 Tbsp curry powder

1/4 cup fresh lime juice

1/2 cup of tomato sauce

2 Tbsp grated ginger

2 cloves of garlic

Salt, to taste

1 cup of canned mushrooms

3 cups coconut milk canned

2 Tbsp fresh chopped mint, to garnish

Instructions

1. Combine ingredients (except coconut milk and mint) in a blender.
2. Blend on high until smooth.
3. Pour in coconut milk, and blend again until combined well.
4. Pour into bowls, sprinkle with fresh mint and serve.
5. Keep refrigerated.

Nutrition Facts

Percent daily values based on the Reference Daily Intake (RDI) for a 2000 calorie diet.

Amount Per Serving

Calories 649.42 | Calories From Fat (85%) 550.12 | Total Fat 64.2g 99% | Saturated Fat 36g 180% | Cholesterol 0mg 0% | Sodium 1361mg 48% | Potassium 934.65mg 27% | Total Carbohydrates 18.3g 6% | Fiber 3.16g 13% | Sugar 4.9g | Protein 10.39g 21%

Slow-Cooked Navy Bean Soup

Ready in Time: 8 hours | Servings: 8

Ingredients

1 lb dry navy beans, soaked, rinsed
4 Tbsp olive oil
1/4 cup onion finely diced
2 cloves garlic finely chopped
2 carrots sliced
1/2 cup tomato sauce (canned)
1 tsp mustard
1/2 tsp curry powder
6 cups of water
Salt and ground black pepper to taste

Instructions

1. Soak beans overnight.
2. Rinse beans and add in your 6 Quart Slow Cooker.
3. Add all remaining ingredients and stir well.
4. Cover and cook on LOW for 8 hours.
5. Adjust the salt and pepper to taste.
6. Serve hot.

Nutrition Facts

Percent daily values based on the Reference Daily Intake (RDI) for a 2000 calorie diet.

Amount Per Serving

Calories 191.2 | Calories From Fat (4%) 7.6 | Total Fat 0.91g 1% | Saturated Fat 0.11g <1% | Cholesterol 0mg 0% | Sodium 146.67mg 6% | Potassium 746.42mg 21% | Total Carbohydrates 35.18g 12% | Fiber 13.64g 55% | Sugar 3.85g | Protein 12.15g 24%

Sour Artichoke Hearts with Rice

Ready in Time: 40 minutes | Servings: 6

Ingredients

1 cup of olive oil
10 canned artichoke hearts, chopped
2 carrots cut into thin slices
1 cup of long-grain rice
3 cups vegetable broth
2 Tbsp of fresh parsley finely chopped
2 Tbsp fresh dill finely chopped
2 Tbsp apple cider vinegar (optional)
Salt and ground pepper to taste

Instructions

1. Heat oil in a large pot over medium-high heat.
2. Add artichokes and sauté for 5 minutes.
3. Add carrots and sprinkle with a pinch of the salt and pepper.
4. Sauté and stir for 2 to 3 minutes.
5. Add rice and stir for one minute.
6. Pour water, and add dill and parsley; stir.
7. Bring to a boil and reduce heat to simmer.
8. Cover and cook for 25 minutes.
9. Taste and adjust seasonings.
10. Pour apple cider vinegar and stir.
11. Serve hot.

Nutrition Facts

Percent daily values based on the Reference Daily Intake (RDI) for a 2000 calorie diet.

Amount Per Serving

Calories 445.53 | Calories From Fat (40%) 180.14 | Total Fat 20.41g 31% | Saturated Fat 3g 15% | Cholesterol 1.23mg <1% | Sodium 1025.47mg 43% | Potassium 854.8mg 24% | Total Carbohydrates 58.7g 20% | Fiber 10.55g 42% | Sugar 1.31g | Protein 11g 22%

Spring Greens and Rice Stew

Ready in Time: 35 minutes | Servings: 4

Ingredients

1/3 cup of olive oil
2 cups lettuce salad, chopped
2 cups dandelion leaves chopped
1 cup rice short grain
3 cups vegetable broth
1 tsp fresh basil finely chopped
2 Tbsp fresh dill chopped
Table salt and ground black pepper to taste

Instructions

1. Heat oil in a large pot over medium-high heat.
2. Sauté lettuce and dandelion leaves for about 4 to 5 minutes.
3. Add rice, cook for one minute; pour rice, and stir.
4. Add in basil, dill, and the salt and ground pepper.
5. Reduce heat to medium-low, cover and cook for about 40 minutes or until all liquid has been absorbed
6. Taste, adjust seasoning, and serve.

Nutrition Facts

Percent daily values based on the Reference Daily Intake (RDI) for a 2000 calorie diet.

Amount Per Serving

Calories 470.95 | Calories From Fat (42%) 199.52 | Total Fat 22.66g 35% | Saturated Fat 3.2g 16% | Cholesterol 1.85mg <1% | Sodium 1246.8mg 52% | Potassium 499mg 14% | Total Carbohydrates 63.81g 21% | Fiber 7g 28% | Sugar 0.2g | Protein 9g 18%

Sweet Potatoes Puree with Almond Milk (Slow Cooker)

Ready in Time: 4 hours and 10 minutes | Servings: 4

Ingredients

2 pounds sweet potatoes peeled and cut into small cubes
1/2 cup almond milk
Pink Himalayan salt
2 Tbsp almond butter
1/4 tsp of turmeric powder
1/2 tsp cinnamon

Instructions

1. Rinse potatoes thoroughly to wash away any dirt.
2. Place sweet potato cubes, almond milk, and a pinch of Pink Himalayan salt in your Slow Cooker.
3. Cover and turn to HIGH 2 hours or on LOW for 4 hours.
4. Transfer potatoes in your fast-speed blender.
5. Add all remaining ingredients.
6. Blend until smooth and creamy.
7. If your puree is too thick, add some more almond milk.
8. Taste and adjust salt to taste.
9. Serve.

Nutrition Facts

Percent daily values based on the Reference Daily Intake (RDI) for a 2000 calorie diet.

Amount Per Serving

Calories 244.98 | Calories From Fat (16%) 38.27 | Total Fat 4.57g 7% | Saturated Fat 0.38g 2% | Cholesterol 0mg 0% | Sodium 184.73mg 8% | Potassium 828mg 24% | Total Carbohydrates 47.31g 16% | Fiber 7.7g 31% | Sugar 9.84g | Protein 5.94g 12%

Tomato Soup with Tagliatelle Pasta

Ready in Time: 45 minutes | Servings: 6

Ingredients

2 Tbsp of olive oil
1 onion finely diced
1 Tbsp sea salt and ground fresh pepper to taste
2 carrots grated
1 Tbsp fresh parsley chopped
1 Tbsp fresh celery chopped
1 pinch ground paprika
1 can (16 oz) tomato crushed
5 cups vegetable broth
1/2 lb Tagliatelle pasta

Instructions

1. Heat oil in a deep and large pot on medium-strong heat.
2. Sauté onion with the pinch of salt until soft; stir.
3. Add crushed tomatoes, parsley, celery, and ground paprika; stir for two minutes.
4. Add all remaining ingredients, stir well, reduce heat to medium, and cook covered for 20 minutes.
5. Add Tagliatelle pasta and cook for about 8 to 11 minutes.
6. Taste, adjust seasonings and serve warm.

Nutrition Facts

Percent daily values based on the Reference Daily Intake (RDI) for a 2000 calorie diet.

Amount Per Serving

Calories 325.58 | Calories From Fat (49%) 158.43 | Total Fat 18.76g 29% | Saturated Fat 2.84g 14% | Cholesterol 0mg 0% | Sodium 372.19mg 16% | Potassium 488.5mg 14% | Total Carbohydrates 34.35g 11% | Fiber 3.65g 15% | Sugar 4.35g |Protein 8.64g 17%

Vegan Brown Rice Stuffed Zucchini

Ready in Time: 1 hour and 5 minutes | Servings: 6

Ingredients

2 lbs zucchini (medium)
1/3 cup avocado oil
1 onion finely chopped
2 cloves garlic finely sliced
1 large carrot cut into small cubes
1 1/4 cups brown rice (uncooked, rinsed and drained)
2 Tbsp arrowroot powder
2 cups vegetable broth
1 Tbsp tomato paste
Salt and ground pepper to taste

Instructions

1. Preheat oven to 360 F/180 C.
2. Slice zucchini in half the long way and use a spoon to scoop out the flesh leaving the thick shell.
3. Grease a baking dish with avocado oil; set aside.
4. Heat oil in a frying skillet, and sauté onion and garlic with the pinch of salt until soft; stir occasionally.
5. Add carrots and stir for about 2 minutes.
6. Add brown rice, arrowroot, vegetable broth, and tomato paste: stir for 3 to 4 minutes.
7. Season with the salt and pepper; stir well.
8. Fill zucchini with the rice mixture and place it into prepared baking dish.
9. Pour little water and cover with the foil.
10. Bake for 45 minutes.
11. Remove foil and allow it to cool for 10 to 15 minutes.
12. Serve.

Nutrition Facts

Percent daily values based on the Reference Daily Intake (RDI) for a 2000 calorie diet.

Amount Per Serving

Calories 161.86 | Calories From Fat (39%) 62.93 | Total Fat 7.2g 11% | Saturated Fat 1g 5% | Cholesterol 0mg 0% | Sodium 116.77mg 5% | Potassium 579.82mg 17% | Total Carbohydrates 21.33g 7% | Fiber 2.59g 10% | Sugar 5.75g | Protein 5g 10%

Vegan Pesto Zucchini Noodles

Ready in Time: 20 minutes | Servings: 2

Ingredients

1 lb zucchini noodles
1/3 cup olive oil
6 cloves garlic minced
1 Tbsp red pepper flakes
1 Tbsp red pepper finely sliced (optional)
Salt and fresh cracked pepper to taste
1/2 cup fresh basil finely chopped
4 Tbsp chopped walnuts

Instructions

1. Cut zucchini into noodle-like strips with a mandoline or grater; drain.
2. In a frying skillet, heat olive oil over medium-high heat.
3. Sauté garlic, red pepper flakes, and red pepper (if used) for one minute.
4. Add zucchini noodles, season with the salt and pepper, and cook for 2 to 3 minutes.
5. Sprinkle with fresh basil; stir slightly and remove from the heat.
6. Serve immediately with chopped walnuts.

Nutrition Facts

Percent daily values based on the Reference Daily Intake (RDI) for a 2000 calorie diet.

Amount Per Serving

Calories 458.96 | Calories From Fat (89%) 406.74 | Total Fat 46.57g 72% | Saturated Fat 6.11g 31% | Cholesterol 0mg 0% | Sodium 20.21mg <1% | Potassium 697.86mg 20% | Total Carbohydrates 9.93g 3% | Fiber 3.79g 15% | Sugar 6.28g | Protein 6g 12%

Vegan Spaghetti with Soy Sauce

Ready in Time: 20 minutes | Servings: 4

Ingredients

1 lb spaghetti
Water for boiling
Garlic Sauce
1/2 cup sesame oil
1/3 cup soy sauce
3 Tbsp garlic minced
1 tsp ground ginger
1 Tbsp brown sugar
1/2 tsp ground cinnamon
Salt and ground black pepper to taste

Instructions

1. Add spaghetti into boiling salted water and cook al dente or for about 8 to 10 minutes.
2. Transfer spaghetti in a colander to drain.
3. In the meantime, prepare the sauce.
4. Heat sesame oil in a saucepan over medium heat.
5. Add all remaining ingredients and cook, stirring occasionally, for about 3 to 4 minutes.
6. Place spaghetti onto a serving plate, and pour evenly with hot sauce.
7. Serve immediately.

Nutrition Facts

Percent daily values based on the Reference Daily Intake (RDI) for a 2000 calorie diet.

Amount Per Serving

Calories 743 | Calories From Fat (35%) 257.34 | Total Fat 29.22g 45% | Saturated Fat 4.24g 21% | Cholesterol 0mg 0% | Sodium 717.51mg 30% | Potassium 360.45mg 10% | Total Carbohydrates 101.7g 34% | Fiber 4.57g 18% | Sugar 7.13g | Protein 18g 36%

White Beans with Herbed Horn Peppers

Ready in Time: 2 hours and 20 minutes | Servings: 6

Ingredients

1 lb white beans soaked

1/2 cup olive oil

1 yellow onion diced

2 red horn peppers cut into slices

3 cloves of garlic finely sliced

1 red horn pepper cut into slices

2 cups vegetable broth

1 cup of water

2 tomatoes, peeled and grated

1 bunch of fresh dill, finely chopped

1 bunch of fresh parsley, finely chopped

Salt and ground pepper to taste

Instructions

1. Soak beans in cold water overnight.
2. In a large pot, heat the olive oil over medium-high heat.
3. Sauté green onions garlic and peppers; stir occasionally.
4. Add white beans and stir well.
5. Pour vegetable broth and water, and stir for about 2 minutes; add grated tomato, salt, pepper, and stir well.
6. Reduce heat to medium-low, cover, and simmer for about 2 hours.
7. After one hour check; if too thick, add some water.
8. Add chopped dill and parsley, stir carefully and adjust salt and pepper to taste.
9. Serve.

Nutrition Facts

Percent daily values based on the Reference Daily Intake (RDI) for a 2000 calorie diet.

Amount Per Serving

Calories 501.65 | Calories From Fat (36%) 178.79 | Total Fat 20.23g 31% | Saturated Fat 3g 15% | Cholesterol 0.82mg <1% | Sodium 661mg 28% | Potassium 1789mg 49% | Total Carbohydrates 62.32g 21% | Fiber 14.93g 60% | Sugar 4.2g | Protein 21.14g 42%

DINNER

Beans and Button Mushrooms "Stew"

Ready in Time: 35 minutes | Servings: 6

Ingredients

4 Tbsp olive oil
1 cup chopped onion
1 tsp minced garlic
1 lb fresh button mushrooms, sliced
3/4 tsp dried thyme, crushed
1 tsp red paprika
2 cups vegetable broth
1 can (11 oz) tomatoes crushed
2 can (15 oz) white beans, drained
Salt and ground black pepper to taste

Instructions

1. Heat olive oil in a pot over medium-high heat.
2. Add onion, garlic, mushrooms, thyme, and red paprika; sauté for about 4 to 5 minutes.
3. Pour the vegetable broth and tomatoes, and bring to a boil.
4. Reduce heat to medium, cover and cook for 15 to 17 minutes
5. Add the beans and stir; cook for a further 2 to 3 minutes.
6. Remove from heat and adjust the salt and pepper to taste.
7. Serve warm.

Nutrition Facts

Percent daily values based on the Reference Daily Intake (RDI) for a 2000 calorie diet.

Amount Per Serving

Calories 347.87 | Calories From Fat (27%) 95.33 | Total Fat 10.82g 17% | Saturated Fat 1.65g 8% | Cholesterol 0.62mg <1% | Sodium 524.34mg 22% | Potassium 1221.5mg 35% | Total Carbohydrates 49g 16% | Fiber 10.43g 42% | Sugar 4.77g | Protein 16.5g 33%

Boosting Black Beans and Avocado Salad

Ready in Time: 15 minutes | Servings: 4

Ingredients

2 can (11 oz) black beans drained
1 avocado cored, cut into cubes
3/4 cup green onions finely chopped
1 cup corn kernels, drained
1 tomato sliced
1 clove garlic finely sliced
1 red bell pepper cut in strips
1 pear cut into cubes
1/2 cup olive oil
1/3 cup fresh lime juice
1/4 tsp salt and ground black pepper to taste
1/2 cup chopped cilantro fresh
2 Tbsp parsley finely chopped

Instructions

1. In a large and deep bowl combine together black beans, avocado, green onion, corn, tomato, garlic, pear, and bell pepper.
2. In a separate bowl, combine all remaining ingredients and pour over black bean mixture.
3. Toss to combine well.
4. Taste and adjust salt and pepper to taste.
5. Serve immediately.

Nutrition Facts

Percent daily values based on the Reference Daily Intake (RDI) for a 2000 calorie diet.

Amount Per Serving

Calories 561.44 | Calories From Fat (54%) 305.11 | Total Fat 34.91g 54% | Saturated Fat 4.87g 24% | Cholesterol 0mg 0% | Sodium 542mg 23% | Potassium 1072.47mg 31% | Total Carbohydrates 54.76g 18% | Fiber 17.1g 71% | Sugar 9.3g | Protein 13.88g 28%

Brown Rice Pasta Salad with Apple Juice Sauce

Ready in Time: 15 minutes | Servings: 4

Ingredients

1 lb Brown rice pasta
1 can (11 oz) corn boiled, drained
1/2 cup chopped red onion
1 cup carrots, shredded
2 roasted red peppers cut into slices or cubes
2 cups mushrooms, sliced
1/2 cup olive oil
1/2 cup apple juice canned or bottled
1/3 cup chopped fresh basil
Salt and freshly ground black pepper

Instructions

1. Prepare pasta according to package directions.
2. Drain pasta and rinse with cold water.
3. Add brown rice pasta into a large salad bowl together with corn, red onion, carrot, peppers, and mushrooms.
4. In a separate bowl, whisk together olive oil, apple juice, basil, and salt and pepper.
5. Pour olive oil sauce over the pasta salad; toss to combine well.
6. Taste and adjust the salt and pepper to taste.
7. Serve or keep refrigerated.

Nutrition Facts

Percent daily values based on the Reference Daily Intake (RDI) for a 2000 calorie diet.

Amount Per Serving

Calories 745.1 | Calories From Fat (33%) 247.48 | Total Fat 28g 43% | Saturated Fat 4g 20% | Cholesterol 0mg 0% | Sodium 185.64mg 8% | Potassium 517.75mg 15% | Total Carbohydrates 105.67g 35% | Fiber 9.16g 37% | Sugar 6.4g | Protein 19g 38%

Garlic -Potato Puree

Ready in Time: 35 minutes | Servings: 6

Ingredients

6 potatoes peeled and halved
Water for cooking
8 cloves of garlic, cleaned
3/4 cup olive oil
2 Tbsp white wine vinegar
Kosher salt and ground white pepper
2 Tbsp fresh parsley chopped for serving

Instructions

1. Peel, cut into halves and rinse potatoes.
2. Cook potatoes in boiling water until tender or about 20 to 25 minutes for halved potatoes.
3. Transfer potatoes in a colander and drain well.
4. Add garlic and olive oil, some salt and pepper in a high-speed blender; blend until combined.
5. Add potatoes and continue to blend until well combined.
6. Remove mixture to a bowl, pour the vinegar and stir with a spoon.
7. Taste and adjust salt and pepper to taste.
8. Sprinkle with chopped parsley and serve!
9. Keep refrigerated.

Nutrition Facts

Percent daily values based on the Reference Daily Intake (RDI) for a 2000 calorie diet.

Amount Per Serving

Calories 413.34 | Calories From Fat (58%) 240.45 | Total Fat 27.21g 42% | Saturated Fat 3.79g 19% | Cholesterol 0mg 0% | Sodium 15.23mg <1% | Potassium 919mg 26% | Total Carbohydrates 39.44g 13% | Fiber 4.77g 19% | Sugar 2.5g | Protein 5g 10%

High Protein Soybean Pasta with Basil

Ready in Time: 35 minutes | Servings: 4

Ingredients

1/2 lb soybean pasta
1 can (11 oz) white bean cooked
4 tsp olive oil
4 tsp garlic finely chopped
1 can (15 oz) tomato crushed
1 can (11 oz) tomato paste
2 tsp dried oregano
Salt and ground black pepper to taste
1/2 cup fresh basil chopped

Instructions

1. Prepare soybean pasta according to package directions; drain.
2. Mash white beans in a blender; set aside.
3. Heat the oil in a saucepan over medium-high heat.
4. Sauté garlic until soft (do not burn it).
5. Add crushed tomatoes and beans, tomato paste, oregano, salt, and pepper.
6. Bring the sauce to a boil, reduce heat to medium-low, and simmer the sauce for 20 minutes.
7. Remove the sauce from the heat and stir in chopped basil.
8. Pour sauce over pasta and serve.

Nutrition Facts

Percent daily values based on the Reference Daily Intake (RDI) for a 2000 calorie diet.

Amount Per Serving

Calories 564.35 | Calories From Fat (10%) 56.26 | Total Fat 6.44g 10% | Saturated Fat 1.04g 5% | Cholesterol 0mg 0% | Sodium 766mg 32% | Potassium 1448mg 38% | Total Carbohydrates 102.47g 34% | Fiber 17.64g 71% | Sugar 11.83g | Protein 29g 58%

Instant Robust Vegan Soup

Ready in Time: 25 minutes | Servings: 8

Ingredients

3 green onions finely chopped
2 cloves crushed garlic
2 carrots sliced into 1/4-inch rounds
Salt and ground black pepper to taste
10 oz fresh spinach chopped
1 cup rice Arborio
3 potatoes cut into large chunks
2 stalk celery cut into 1-inch chunks
4 cups vegetable broth
4 Tbsp olive oil
1 cup fresh parsley (chopped)
2 Tbsp fresh celery (chopped)
2 Tbsp fresh lemon juice
2 Tbsp tomato paste
1 bay leaf

Instructions

1. Press the SAUTÉ button on your Instant Pot.
2. When the word "hot" appears on display, add oil and sauté onions, garlic, and carrots, occasionally stirring for about 5 minutes.
3. Add rice and potatoes; sauté for one to two minutes.
4. Add all remaining ingredients and give a good stir.
5. Lock lid into place and set on the MANUAL on High pressure for 12 minutes.
6. When the timer beeps, press "Cancel" and carefully flip the Quick Release valve to let the pressure out.
7. Once all of the pressure releases, the steam will no longer come out of the vent carefully open the lid.
8. Taste and adjust seasonings.
9. Serve hot.

Nutrition Facts

Percent daily values based on the Reference Daily Intake (RDI) for a 2000 calorie diet.

Amount Per Serving

Calories 317.26 | Calories From Fat (26%) 82.69 | Total Fat 9.37g 14% | Saturated Fat 1.48g 7% | Cholesterol 1.23mg <1% | Sodium 1304.4mg 54% | Potassium 869.14mg 25% | Total Carbohydrates 51.38g 17% | Fiber 6.13g 25% | Sugar 3.2g | Protein 9g 18%

Instant Savory Gigante Beans

Ready in Time: 55 minutes | Servings: 6

Ingredients

1 lb Gigante Beans soaked overnight

1/2 cup olive oil

1 onion sliced

2 cloves garlic crushed or minced

1 red bell pepper (cut into 1/2-inch pieces)

2 carrots, sliced

1/2 tsp salt and ground black pepper

2 tomatoes peeled, grated

1 Tbsp celery (chopped)

1 Tbsp tomato paste (or ketchup)

3/4 tsp sweet paprika

1 tsp oregano

1 cup vegetable broth

Instructions

1. Soak Gigante beans overnight.
2. Press SAUTÉ button on your Instant Pot and heat the oil.
3. Sauté onion, garlic, sweet pepper, carrots with a pinch of salt for 3 - 4 minutes; stir occasionally.
4. Add rinsed Gigante beans into your Instant Pot along with all remaining ingredients and stir well.
5. Lock lid into place and set on the MANUAL setting for 25 minutes.
6. When the beep sounds, quick release the pressure by pressing Cancel, and twisting the steam handle to the Venting position.
7. Taste and adjust seasonings to taste.
8. Serve warm or cold.
9. Keep refrigerated.

Nutrition Facts

Percent daily values based on the Reference Daily Intake (RDI) for a 2000 calorie diet.

Amount Per Serving

Calories 502.45 | Calories From Fat (34%) 173.16 | Total Fat 19.63g 30% | Saturated Fat 2.86g 14% | Cholesterol 0.41mg <1% | Sodium 326.4mg 14% | Potassium 1869.29mg 53% | Total Carbohydrates 63.17g 21% | Fiber 15.63g 63% | Sugar 6.37g | Protein 21.74g 44%

Instant Turmeric Risotto

Ready in Time: 40 minutes | Servings: 4

Ingredients

4 Tbsp olive oil
1 cup onion
1 tsp minced garlic
2 cups long-grain rice
3 cups vegetable broth
1/2 tsp paprika (smoked)
1/2 tsp turmeric
1/2 tsp nutmeg
2 Tbsp fresh basil leaves chopped
Salt and ground black pepper to taste

Instructions

1. Press the SAUTÉ button on your Instant Pot and heat oil.
2. Sauté the onion and garlic with a pinch of salt until softened.
3. Add the rice and all remaining ingredients and stir well.
4. Lock lid into place and set on and select the "RICE" button for 10 minutes.
5. When the timer beeps, press "Cancel" and carefully flip the Quick Release valve to let the pressure out.
6. Taste and adjust seasonings to taste.
7. Serve.

Nutrition Facts

Percent daily values based on the Reference Daily Intake (RDI) for a 2000 calorie diet.

Amount Per Serving

Calories 559.81 | Calories From Fat (29%) 162.48 | Total Fat 18.57g 29% | Saturated Fat 2.4g 12% | Cholesterol 1.23mg <1% | Sodium 815.34mg 34% | Potassium 26.6mg 7% | Total Carbohydrates 97.3g 32% | Fiber 8.43g 34% | Sugar 1.81g | Protein 10g 20%

Nettle Soup with Rice

Ready in Time: 40 minutes | Servings: 5

Ingredients

3 Tbsp of olive oil
2 onions finely chopped
2 cloves garlic finely chopped
Salt and freshly ground black pepper
4 medium potatoes cut into cubes
1 cup of rice
1 Tbsp arrowroot
2 cups vegetable broth
2 cups of water
1 bunch of young nettle leaves packed
1/2 cup fresh parsley finely chopped
1 tsp cumin

Instructions

1. Heat olive oil in a large pot.
2. Sauté onion and garlic with a pinch of salt until softened.
3. Add potato, rice, and arrowroot; sauté for 2 to 3 minutes.
4. Pour broth and water, stir well, cover and cook over medium heat for about 20 minutes.
5. Cook over medium heat for about 20 minutes.
6. Add young nettle leaves, parsley, and cumin; stir and cook for 5 to 7 minutes.
7. Transfer the soup in a blender and blend until combined well.
8. Taste and adjust salt and pepper.
9. Serve hot.

Nutrition Facts

Percent daily values based on the Reference Daily Intake (RDI) for a 2000 calorie diet.

Amount Per Serving

Calories 421.76 | Calories From Fat (21%) 88.32 | Total Fat 9.8g 15% | Saturated Fat 1.54g 8% | Cholesterol 0.8mg <1% | Sodium 790.86mg 33% | Potassium 963.6mg 28% | Total Carbohydrates 73.52g 25% | Fiber 8g 32% | Sugar 3.3g | Protein 9.66g 19%

Okra with Grated Tomatoes (Slow Cooker)

Ready in Time: 3 hours and 10 minutes | Servings: 4

Ingredients

2 lbs fresh okra cleaned
2 onions finely chopped
2 cloves garlic finely sliced
2 carrots sliced
2 ripe tomatoes grated
1 cup of water
4 Tbsp olive oil
Salt and ground black pepper
1 Tbsp fresh parsley finely chopped

Instructions

1. Add okra in your Crock-Pot: sprinkle with a pinch of salt and pepper.
2. Add in chopped onion, garlic, carrots, and grated tomatoes; stir well.
3. Pour water and oil, season with the salt, pepper, and give a good stir.
4. Cover and cook on LOW for 2-3 hours or until tender.
5. Open the lid and add fresh parsley; stir.
6. Taste and adjust salt and pepper.
7. Serve hot.

Nutrition Facts

Percent daily values based on the Reference Daily Intake (RDI) for a 2000 calorie diet.

Amount Per Serving

Calories 223.47 | Calories From Fat (55%) 123.5 | Total Fat 14g 22% | Saturated Fat 1.96g 10% | Cholesterol 0mg 0% | Sodium 51.91mg 2% | Potassium 1009.6mg 29% | Total Carbohydrates 23.58g 8% | Fiber 9.47g 38% | Sugar 6.62g | Protein 6g 12%

Oven-baked Smoked Lentil 'Burgers'

Ready in Time: 1 hour and 20 minutes | Servings: 6

Ingredients

1 1/2 cups dried lentils
3 cups of water
Salt and ground black pepper to taste
2 Tbsp olive oil
1 onion finely diced
2 cloves minced garlic
1 cup button mushrooms sliced
2 Tbsp tomato paste
1/2 tsp fresh basil finely chopped
1 cup chopped almonds
3 tsp balsamic vinegar
3 Tbsp coconut aminos
1 tsp liquid smoke
3/4 cup silken tofu soft
3/4 cup corn starch

Instructions

1. Cook lentils in salted water until tender or for about 30-35 minutes; rinse, drain, and set aside.
2. Heat oil in a frying skillet and sauté onion, garlic and mushrooms for 4 to 5 minutes; stir occasionally.
3. Stir in the tomato paste, salt, basil, salt, and black pepper; cook for 2 to 3 minutes.
4. Stir in almonds, vinegar, coconut aminos, liquid smoke, and lentils.
5. Remove from heat and stir in blended tofu and corn starch.
6. Keep stirring until all ingredients combined well.
7. Form mixture into patties and refrigerate for an hour.
8. Preheat oven to 350 F.
9. Line a baking dish with parchment paper and arrange patties on the pan.
10. Bake for 20 to 25 minutes.
11. Serve hot with buns, green salad, tomato sauce...etc.

Nutrition Facts

Percent daily values based on the Reference Daily Intake (RDI) for a 2000 calorie diet.

Amount Per Serving

Calories 439.12 | Calories From Fat (34%) 148.97 | Total Fat 17.48g 27% | Saturated Fat 1.71g 9% | Cholesterol 0mg 0% | Sodium 330mg 14% | Potassium 805.8mg 23% | Total Carbohydrates 53.72g 18% | Fiber 18.19g 73% | Sugar 4.6g | Protein 19.37g 39%

Powerful Spinach and Mustard Leaves Puree

Ready in Time: 50 minutes | Servings: 4

Ingredients

2 Tbsp almond butter
1 onion finely diced
2 Tbsp minced garlic
1 tsp salt and black pepper (or to taste)
1 lb mustard leaves, cleaned rinsed
1 lb frozen spinach thawed
1 tsp coriander
1 tsp ground cumin
1/2 cup almond milk

Instructions

1. Press the SAUTÉ button on your Instant Pot and heat the almond butter.
2. Sauté onion, garlic, and a pinch of salt for 2-3 minutes; stir occasionally.
3. Add spinach and the mustard greens and stir for a minute or two.
4. Season with the salt and pepper, coriander, and cumin; give a good stir.
5. Lock lid into place and set on the MANUAL setting for 15 minutes.
6. Use Quick Release - turn the valve from sealing to venting to release the pressure.
7. Transfer mixture to a blender, add almond milk and blend until smooth.
8. Taste and adjust seasonings.
9. Serve.

Nutrition Facts

Percent daily values based on the Reference Daily Intake (RDI) for a 2000 calorie diet.

Amount Per Serving

Calories 180.53 | Calories From Fat (46%) 82.69 | Total Fat 10g 15% | Saturated Fat 0.65g 3% | Cholesterol 0mg 0% | Sodium 1519.12mg 63% | Potassium 846mg 24% | Total Carbohydrates 17.46g 6% | Fiber 6.92g 28% | Sugar 2.13g | Protein 10.65g 21%

Quinoa and Rice Stuffed Peppers (oven-baked)

Ready in Time: 35 minutes | Servings: 8

Ingredients

3/4 cup long-grain rice
8 bell peppers (any color)
2 Tbsp olive oil
1 onion finely diced
2 cloves chopped garlic
1 can (11 oz) crushed tomatoes
1 tsp cumin
1 tsp coriander
4 Tbsp ground walnuts
2 cups cooked quinoa
4 Tbsp chopped parsley
Salt and ground black pepper to taste

Instructions

1. Preheat oven to 400 F/200 C.
2. Boil rice and drain in a colander.
3. Cut the top stem section of the pepper off, remove the remaining pith and seeds, rinse peppers.
4. Heat oil in a large frying skillet, and sauté onion and garlic until soft.
5. Add tomatoes, cumin, ground almonds, salt, pepper, and coriander; stir well and simmer for 2 minutes stirring constantly.
6. Remove from the heat and add the rice, quinoa, and parsley; stir well.
7. Taste and adjust salt and pepper.
8. Fill the peppers with a mixture, and place peppers cut side-up in a baking dish; drizzle with little oil.
9. Bake for 15 minutes.
10. Serve warm.

Nutrition Facts

Percent daily values based on the Reference Daily Intake (RDI) for a 2000 calorie diet.

Amount Per Serving

Calories 335.69 | Calories From Fat (25%) 83.63 | Total Fat 9.58g 15% | Saturated Fat 1.2g 5% | Cholesterol 0mg 0% | Sodium 66.14mg 3% | Potassium 678.73mg 19% | Total Carbohydrates 55.13g 18% | Fiber 8.25g 33% | Sugar 7.8g | Protein 9.8g 20%

Quinoa and Lentils with Crushed Tomato

Ready in Time: 35 minutes | Servings: 4

Ingredients

4 Tbsp olive oil

1 medium onion, diced

2 garlic clove, minced

Salt and ground black pepper to taste

1 can (15 oz) tomatoes crushed

1 cup vegetable broth

1/2 cup quinoa, washed and drained

1 cup cooked lentils

1 tsp chili powder

1 tsp cumin

Instructions

1. Heat oil in a pot and sauté the onion and garlic with the pinch of salt until soft.
2. Pour reserved tomatoes and vegetable broth, bring to boil, and stir well.
3. Stir in the quinoa, cover and cook for 15 minutes; stir occasionally.
4. Add in lentils, chili powder, and cumin; cook for further 5 minutes.
5. Taste and adjust seasonings.
6. Serve immediately.
7. Keep refrigerated in a covered container for 4 - 5 days.

Nutrition Facts

Percent daily values based on the Reference Daily Intake (RDI) for a 2000 calorie diet.

Amount Per Serving

Calories 397.45 | Calories From Fat (35%) 138.18 | Total Fat 15.61g 24% | Saturated Fat 2.14g 11% | Cholesterol 0mg 0% | Sodium 343.8mg 14% | Potassium 738.51mg 21% | Total Carbohydrates 49.32g 16% | Fiber 16.7g 68% | Sugar 2.35g | Protein 16.6g 33%

Silk Tofu Penne with Spinach

Ready in Time: 25 minutes | Servings: 4

Ingredients

1 lb penne, uncooked
12 oz of frozen spinach, thawed
1 cup silken tofu mashed
1/2 cup soy milk (unsweetened)
1/2 cup vegetable broth
1 Tbsp white wine vinegar
1/2 tsp Italian seasoning
Salt and ground pepper to taste

Instructions

1. Cook penne pasta according to package directions; rinse and drain in a colander.
2. Drain spinach well, squeezing out excess liquid.
3. Place spinach with all remaining ingredients in a blender and beat until smooth.
4. Pour the spinach mixture over pasta.
5. Taste and adjust the salt and pepper.
6. Store pasta in an airtight container in the refrigerator for 3 to 5 days.

Nutrition Facts

Percent daily values based on the Reference Daily Intake (RDI) for a 2000 calorie diet.

Amount Per Serving

Calories 492.8 | Calories From Fat (5%) 27.06 | Total Fat 3.07g 5% | Saturated Fat 0.38g 2% | Cholesterol 0.31mg <1% | Sodium 491.22mg 20% | Potassium 433mg 12% | Total Carbohydrates 92.45g 31% | Fiber 7.8g 31% | Sugar 1.21g | Protein 21.61g 43%

Slow-Cooked Butter Beans, Okra and Potatoes Stew

Ready in Time: 6 hours and 5 minutes | Servings: 6

Ingredients

2 cups frozen butter (lima) beans, thawed
1 cup frozen okra, thawed
2 large Russet potatoes cut into cubes
1 can (6 oz) whole-kernel corn, drained
1 large carrot sliced
1 green bell pepper finely chopped
1 cup green peas
1/2 cup chopped celery
1 medium onion finely chopped
2 cups vegetable broth
2 cans (6 oz) tomato sauce
1 cup of water
1/2 tsp salt and freshly ground black pepper

Instructions

1. Combine all ingredients in your Slow Cooker; give a good stir.
2. Cover and cook on HIGH for 6 hours.
3. Taste, adjust seasonings, and serve hot.

Nutrition Facts

Percent daily values based on the Reference Daily Intake (RDI) for a 2000 calorie diet.

Amount Per Serving

Calories 241.71 | Calories From Fat (5%) 11.22 | Total Fat 1.28g 2% | Saturated Fat 0.27g 1% | Cholesterol 0mg 0% | Sodium 714.16mg 30% | Potassium 1228mg 35 % | Total Carbohydrates 49.6g 17% | Fiber 9.65g 39% | Sugar 8.17g | Protein 10.57g 21%

Soya Minced Stuffed Eggplants

Ready in Time: 1 hour | Servings: 4

Ingredients

2 eggplants
1/3 cup sesame oil
1 onion finely chopped
2 garlic cloves minced
1 lb soya mince* see note
Salt and ground black pepper
1/3 cup almond milk
2 Tbsp fresh parsley, chopped
1/3 cup fresh basil chopped
1 tsp fennel powder
1 cup of water
4 Tbsp tomato paste (fresh or canned)

Instructions

1. Rinse and slice the eggplant in half lengthwise.
2. Submerge sliced eggplant into a container with salted water.
3. Soak soya mince in water for 10 to 15 minutes.
4. Preheat oven to 400 F.
5. Rinse eggplant and dry with a clean towel.
6. Heat oil in large frying skillet, and sauté onion and garlic with a pinch of salt until softened.
7. Add drained soya mince, and cook over medium heat until cooked through.
8. Add all remaining ingredients (except water and tomato paste) and cook for a further 5 minutes; remove from heat.
9. Scoop out the seed part of each eggplant.
10. Spoon in the filling and arrange stuffed eggplants onto the large baking dish.
11. Dissolve tomato paste into the water and pour evenly over eggplants.
12. Bake for 20 to 25 minutes.
13. Serve warm.

Nutrition Facts

Percent daily values based on the Reference Daily Intake (RDI) for a 2000 calorie diet.

Amount Per Serving

Calories 287.32 | Calories From Fat (49%) 141.77 | Total Fat 16.42g 25% | Saturated Fat 2.02g 10% | Cholesterol 0mg 0% | Sodium 104.72mg 4% | Potassium 1150.5mg 33% | Total Carbohydrates 24.67g 8% | Fiber 11.16g 45% | Sugar 4.75g | Protein 16.16g 32%

Notes: Soya mince is made from soy flour and may be left plain or flavored to mimic chicken, sausage, or ground beef.

Triple Beans and Corn Salad

Ready in Time: 15 minutes | Servings: 8

Ingredients

1 can (15 oz) kidney beans, drained and rinsed
1 can (15 oz) white beans, drained and rinsed
1 can (15 oz) black beans, rinsed and drained
1 can (11 oz) frozen corn kernels thawed
1 green bell pepper, chopped
1 red onion, chopped
1 clove crushed garlic
1 Tbsp salt and ground black pepper to taste
1/2 cup olive oil
3 Tbsp red wine vinegar
3 Tbsp lemon juice
1/4 cup chopped fresh cilantro
1/2 Tbsp ground cumin

Instructions

1. In a large bowl, combine beans, corn, pepper, onion, and garlic.
2. Season salad with the salt and pepper; stir to combine well.
3. In a separate bowl, whisk together olive oil, red wine vinegar, lemon juice, cilantro, and cumin.
4. Pour olive oil dressing over salad, and toss to combine well.
5. Refrigerate for one hour and serve.

Nutrition Facts

Percent daily values based on the Reference Daily Intake (RDI) for a 2000 calorie diet.

Amount Per Serving

Calories 696 | Calories From Fat (22%) 155.25 | Total Fat 17.62g 27% | Saturated Fat 3g 15% | Cholesterol 0mg 0% | Sodium 1118mg 47% | Potassium 1719.68mg 48% | Total Carbohydrates 102.9g 34% | Fiber 25g 102% | Sugar 1.68g | Protein 36.94g 74%

Vegan Raw Pistachio Flaxseed 'Burgers'

Ready in Time: 15 minutes | Servings: 4

Ingredients

1 cup ground flaxseed
1 cup pistachio finely sliced
2 cups cooked spinach drained
2 Tbsp sesame oil
4 cloves garlic finely sliced
2 Tbsp lemon juice, freshly squeezed
Sea salt to taste

Instructions

1. Add all ingredients into a food processor or high-speed blender; process until combined well.
2. Form mixture into patties.
3. Refrigerate for one hour.
4. Serve with your favorite vegetable dip.

Nutrition Facts

Percent daily values based on the Reference Daily Intake (RDI) for a 2000 calorie diet.

Amount Per Serving

Calories 273 | Calories From Fat (68%) 184.41 | Total Fat 21.6g 33% | Saturated Fat 2.72g 14% | Cholesterol 0mg 0% | Sodium 322.9mg 13% | Potassium 637mg 18% | Total Carbohydrates 14.8g 5% | Fiber 7g 28% | Sugar 3.1g | Protein 10.46g 21%

Vegan Red Bean 'Fricassee'

Ready in Time: 40 minutes | Servings: 4

Ingredients

4 Tbsp olive oil

1 onion finely sliced

2 cloves garlic finely chopped

Salt and freshly ground black pepper to taste

1 can (15 oz) red beans

1 large carrot grated

1 1/2 cup vegetable broth

1 cup of water

1 can (6 oz) tomato paste

1 tsp ground paprika

1 tsp parsley

Instructions

1. Heat oil in a large pot and sauté onion and garlic with a pinch of salt until soft.
2. Add red beans together with all remaining ingredients and stir well.
3. In a separate pan, sauté onion and garlic in the olive oil.
4. Reduce heat to medium, and simmer for 25 to 30 minutes.
5. Taste and adjust salt and pepper if needed.
6. Serve hot.

Nutrition Facts

Percent daily values based on the Reference Daily Intake (RDI) for a 2000 calorie diet.

Amount Per Serving

Calories 318.72 | Calories From Fat (43%) 136.25 | Total Fat 15.44g 24% | Saturated Fat 2.31g 12% | Cholesterol 0.77mg <1% | Sodium 1136.22mg 47% | Potassium 954.73mg 27% | Total Carbohydrates 38.4g 13% | Fiber 9.81g 39% | Sugar 9.49g | Protein 10g 20%

SNACKS

Beans with Sesame Hummus

Ready in Time: 10 minutes | Servings: 6

Ingredients

4 Tbsp sesame oil
2 cloves garlic finely sliced
1 can (15 oz) cannellini beans, drained
4 Tbsp sesame paste
2 Tbsp lemon juice freshly squeezed
1/4 tsp red pepper flakes
2 Tbsp fresh basil finely chopped
2 Tbsp fresh parsley finely chopped
Sea salt to taste

Instructions

1. Place all ingredients in your food processor.
2. Process until all ingredients are combined well and smooth.
3. Transfer mixture into a bowl and refrigerate until servings.

Nutrition Facts

Percent daily values based on the Reference Daily Intake (RDI) for a 2000 calorie diet.

Amount Per Serving

Calories 491.59 | Calories From Fat (74%) 365.15 | Total Fat 43.14g 66% | Saturated Fat 6.09g 30% | Cholesterol 0mg 0% | Sodium 108.39mg 5% | Potassium 521.26mg 15% | Total Carbohydrates 20.71g 7% | Fiber 6g 23% | Sugar 0.73g | Protein 13.33g 27%

Candied Honey-Coconut Peanuts

Ready in Time: 15 minutes | Servings: 8

Ingredients

1/2 cup honey (preferably a darker honey)
4 Tbsp coconut butter softened
1 tsp ground cinnamon
4 cups roasted, salted peanuts

Instructions

1. Add honey, coconut butter, and cinnamon in a microwave-safe bowl.
2. Microwave at HIGH for about 4 to 5 minutes.
3. Stir in nuts; mix thoroughly to coat.
4. Microwave at HIGH 5 to 6 minutes or until foamy; stir after 3 minutes.
5. Spread in a single layer on a greased tray.
6. Refrigerated for 6 hours.
7. Break into small pieces and serve.

Nutrition Facts

Percent daily values based on the Reference Daily Intake (RDI) for a 2000 calorie diet.

Amount Per Serving

Calories 550.88 | Calories From Fat (66%) 361.89 | Total Fat 43g 66% | Saturated Fat 10.92g 55% | Cholesterol 0mg 0% | Sodium 5.26mg <1% | Potassium 492.76mg 14% | Total Carbohydrates 33.42g 11% | Fiber 6g 24% | Sugar 20.46g | Protein 17.36g 35%

Choco Walnuts Fat Bombs

Preparation Time: 15 minutes | Servings: 6

Ingredients

1/2 cup coconut butter
1/2 cup coconut oil softened
4 Tbs cocoa powder, unsweetened
4 Tbs brown sugar firmly packed
1/3 cup silken tofu mashed
1 cup walnuts, roughly chopped

Instructions

1. Add coconut butter and coconut oil into a microwave dish; melt it for 10-15 seconds.
2. Add in cocoa powder and whisk well.
3. Pour mixture into a blender with brown sugar and silken tofu cream; blend for 3-4 minutes.
4. Place silicone molds onto a sheet pan and fill halfway with chopped walnuts.
5. Pour the mixture over the walnuts and place it in the freezer for 6 hours.
6. Ready! Serve!

Nutrition Facts

Percent daily values based on the Reference Daily Intake (RDI) for a 2000 calorie diet.

Amount Per Serving

Calories 506 | Calories From Fat (86%) 435.7 | Total Fat 50.44g 78% | Saturated Fat 28.16g 141% | Cholesterol 0mg 0% | Sodium 5.38mg <1% | Potassium 213mg 6% | Total Carbohydrates 14.72g 5% | Fiber 2.54g 10% | Sugar 9g | Protein 5.29g 11%

Crispy Honey Pecans (Slow Cooker)

Ready in Time: 2 hours and 15 minutes | Servings: 4

Ingredients

16 oz pecan halves
4 Tbsp coconut butter melted
4 to 5 Tbsp honey strained
1/4 tsp ground ginger
1/4 tsp ground allspice
1 1/2 tsp ground cinnamon

Instructions

1. Add pecans and melted coconut butter into your 4-quart Slow Cooker.
2. Stir until combined well.
3. Add in honey and stir well.
4. In a bowl, combine spices and sprinkle over nuts; stir lightly.
5. Cook on LOW uncovered for about 2 to 3 hours or until nuts are crispy.
6. Serve cold.

Nutrition Facts

Percent daily values based on the Reference Daily Intake (RDI) for a 2000 calorie diet.

Amount Per Serving

Calories 852 | Calories From Fat (82%) 784.5 | Total Fat 93.15g 143% | Saturated Fat 14,31g 72% | Cholesterol 30.53mg 10% | Sodium 2.61mg <1% | Potassium 485.23mg 14% | Total Carbohydrates 33.2g 11% | Fiber 11.47g 46% | Sugar 21.78g | Protein 10.63g 21%

Crunchy Fried Pickles

Ready in Time: 5 minutes | Servings: 6

Ingredients

1/2 cup Vegetable oil for frying
1 cup all-purpose flour
1 cup plain breadcrumbs
Pinch of salt and pepper
30 pickle chips (cucumber, dill)

Instructions

1. Heat oil in a large frying skillet over medium-high heat.
2. Stir the flour, breadcrumbs, and the salt and pepper in a shallow bowl.
3. Dredge the pickles in the flour/breadcrumbs mixture to coat completely.
4. Fry in batches until golden brown on all sides, 2 to 3 minutes in total.
5. Drain on paper towels and serve.

Nutrition Facts

Percent daily values based on the Reference Daily Intake (RDI) for a 2000 calorie diet.

Amount Per Serving

Calories 328.53 | Calories From Fat (53%) 172.76 | Total Fat 19.57g 30% | Saturated Fat 1.65g 8% | Cholesterol 0mg 0% | Sodium 1063.43mg 49% | Potassium 218.57mg 6% | Total Carbohydrates 33.39g 11% | Fiber 3.3g 13% | Sugar 3.46g | Protein 5.61g 11%

Granola bars with Maple Syrup

Ready in Time: 15 minutes | Servings: 12

Ingredients

3/4 cup dates chopped
2 Tbsp chia seeds soaked
3/4 cup rolled oats
4 Tbsp Chopped nuts such Macadamia, almond, Brazilian...etc,
2 Tbsp shredded coconut
2 Tbsp pumpkin seeds
2 Tbsp sesame seeds
2 Tbsp hemp seeds
1/2 cup maple syrup (or to taste)
1/4 cup peanut butter

Instructions

1. Add all ingredients (except maple syrup and peanut butter) into a food processor and pulse just until roughly combined.
2. Add maple syrup and peanut butter and process until all ingredients are combined well.
3. Place baking paper onto a medium baking dish and spread the mixture.
4. Cover with a plastic wrap and press down to make it flat.
5. Chill granola in the fridge for one hour.
6. Cut it into 12 bars and serve.
7. Keep stored in an airtight container for up to 1 week.
8. Also, you can wrap them individually in parchment paper, and keep in the freezer in a large Ziploc bag.

Nutrition Facts

Percent daily values based on the Reference Daily Intake (RDI) for a 2000 calorie diet.

Amount Per Serving

Calories 222.37 | Calories From Fat (48%) 107 | Total Fat 12.79g 20% | Saturated Fat 2.25g 11% | Cholesterol 0mg 0% | Sodium 44.74mg 2% | Potassium 212.28mg 6% | Total Carbohydrates 26.11g 9% | Fiber 4.69g 19% | Sugar 16.25g | Protein 4.19g 8%

Green Soy Beans Hummus

Ready in Time: 15 minutes | Servings: 6

Ingredients

1 1/2 cups frozen green soybeans
4 cups of water
coarse salt to taste
1/4 cup sesame paste
1/2 tsp grated lemon peel
3 Tbsp fresh lemon juice
2 cloves of garlic crushed
1/2 tsp ground cumin
1/4 tsp ground coriander
4 Tbsp extra virgin olive oil
1 Tbsp fresh parsley leaves chopped
Serving options: sliced cucumber, celery, olives

Instructions

1. In a saucepan, bring to boil 4 cups of water with 2 to 3 pinch of coarse salt.
2. Add in frozen soybeans, and cook for 5 minutes or until tender.
3. Rinse and drain soybeans into a colander.
4. Add soybeans and all remaining ingredients into a food processor.
5. Pulse until smooth and creamy.
6. Taste and adjust salt to taste.
7. Serve with sliced cucumber, celery, olives, bread...etc.

Nutrition Facts

Percent daily values based on the Reference Daily Intake (RDI) for a 2000 calorie diet.

Amount Per Serving

Calories 235 | Calories From Fat (67%) 156.89 | Total Fat 18.23g 28% | Saturated Fat 2.43g 12% | Cholesterol 0mg 0% | Sodium 18.71mg <1% | Potassium 458.22mg 13% | Total Carbohydrates 10.73g 4% | Fiber 3.75g 15% | Sugar 0.22g | Protein 10.22g 20%

High Protein Avocado Guacamole

Ready in Time: 15 minutes | Servings: 4

Ingredients

1/2 cup of onion, finely chopped
1 chili pepper (peeled and finely chopped)
1 cup tomato, finely chopped
Cilantro leaves, fresh
2 avocados
2 Tbsp linseed oil
1/2 cup ground walnuts
1/2 lemon (or lime)
Salt

Instructions

1. Chop the onion, chili pepper, cilantro, and tomato; place in a large bowl.
2. Slice avocado, open vertically, and remove the pit.
3. Using the spoon take out the avocado flesh.
4. Mash the avocados with a fork and add into the bowl with onion mixture.
5. Add all remaining ingredients and stir well until ingredients combine well.
6. Taste and adjust salt and lemon/lime juice.
7. Keep refrigerated into covered glass bowl up to 5 days.

Nutrition Facts

Percent daily values based on the Reference Daily Intake (RDI) for a 2000 calorie diet.

Amount Per Serving

Calories 424.8 | Calories From Fat (49%) 209.38 | Total Fat 25.18g 39% | Saturated Fat 2.6g 13% | Cholesterol 0mg 0% | Sodium 19.42mg <1% | Potassium 1580mg 45% | Total Carbohydrates 50.2g 17% | Fiber 10g 40% | Sugar 19.1g | Protein 12.52g 25%

Homemade Energy Nut Bars

Ready in Time: 15 minutes | Servings: 4

Ingredients

1/2 cup peanuts
1 cup almonds
1/2 cup hazelnut, chopped
1 cup shredded coconut
1 cup almond butter
2 tsp sesame seeds toasted
1/2 cup coconut oil, freshly melted
2 Tbsp organic honey
1/4 tsp cinnamon

Instructions

1. Add all nuts into a food processor and pulse for 1-2 minutes.
2. Add in shredded coconut, almond butter, sesame seeds, melted coconut oil, cinnamon, and honey; process only for one minute.
3. Cover a square plate/tray with parchment paper and apply the nut mixture.
4. Spread mixture vigorously with a spatula.
5. Place in the freezer for 4 hours or overnight.
6. Remove from the freezer and cut into rectangular bars.
7. Ready! Enjoy!

Nutrition Facts

Percent daily values based on the Reference Daily Intake (RDI) for a 2000 calorie diet.

Amount Per Serving

Calories 750.82 | Calories From Fat (79%) 594.13 | Total Fat 70.18g 108% | Saturated Fat 29.6g 150% | Cholesterol 0mg 0% | Sodium 66.47mg 3% | Potassium 576.7mg 16% | Total Carbohydrates 26.54g 9% | Fiber 8.18g 33% | Sugar 13.1g | Protein 14.48g 29%

Honey Peanut Butter

Ready in Time: 10 minutes | Servings: 6

Ingredients

1 cup peanut butter
3/4 cup honey extracted
1/2 cup ground peanuts
1 tsp ground cinnamon

Instructions

1. Add all ingredients into your fast-speed blender, and blend until smooth.
2. Keep refrigerated.

Nutrition Facts

Percent daily values based on the Reference Daily Intake (RDI) for a 2000 calorie diet.

Amount Per Serving

Calories 453,91 | Calories From Fat (51%) 231,81 | Total Fat 27.72g 43% | Saturated Fat 5.36g 27% | Cholesterol 0mg 0% | Sodium 199.4mg 8% | Potassium 383mg 11% | Total Carbohydrates 46.29g 15% | Fiber 3.87g 15% | Sugar 39.28g | Protein 13.81g 28%

Mediterranean Marinated Olives

Preparation Time: 10 minutes | Servings: 2

Ingredients

24 large olives, black, green, Kalamata
1/2 cup extra-virgin olive oil
4 cloves garlic, thinly sliced
2 Tbsp fresh lemon juice
2 tsp coriander seeds, crushed
1/2 tsp crushed red pepper
1 tsp dried thyme
1 tsp dried rosemary, crushed
Salt and ground pepper to taste

Instructions

1. Place olives and all remaining ingredients in a large container or bag, and shake to combine well.
2. Cover and refrigerate to marinate overnight.
3. Serve.
4. Keep refrigerated.

Nutrition Facts

Percent daily values based on the Reference Daily Intake (RDI) for a 2000 calorie diet.

Amount Per Serving

Calories 573.31 | Calories From Fat (94%) 540 | Total Fat 61.36g 94% | Saturated Fat 8.41g 42% | Cholesterol 0mg 0% | Sodium 578.6mg 24% | Potassium 76.4mg 2% | Total Carbohydrates 8.6g 3% | Fiber 3.33g 13% | Sugar 0.46g | Protein 1.18g 2%

Nut Butter & Dates Granola

Ready in Time: 1 hour | Servings: 8

Ingredients

3 cups rolled oats
2 cups dates, pitted and chopped
1 cup flaked or shredded coconut
1/2 cup wheat germ
1/4 cup soy milk powder
1/2 cup almonds chopped
3/4 cup honey strained
1/2 cup almond butter (plain, unsalted) softened
1/4 cup peanut butter softened

Instructions

1. Preheat oven to 300F.
2. Add all ingredients into a food processor and pulse until roughly combined.
3. Spread mixture evenly into greased 10 x 15-inch baking pan.
4. Bake for 45 to 55 minutes.
5. Stir mixture several times during baking.
6. Remove from the oven and cool completely.
7. Store in a covered glass jar.

Nutrition Facts

Percent daily values based on the Reference Daily Intake (RDI) for a 2000 calorie diet.

Amount Per Serving

Calories 586 | Calories From Fat (30%) 177.61 | Total Fat 21.22g 33% | Saturated Fat 4.64g 23% | Cholesterol 0mg 0% | Sodium 72.47mg 3% | Potassium 734.14mg 21% | Total Carbohydrates 94.85g 32% | Fiber 11.41g 46% | Sugar 56g | Protein 13.9g 28%

Oven-baked Caramelize Plantains

Ready in Time: 30 minutes | Servings: 4

Ingredients

4 medium plantains, peeled and sliced

2 Tbsp fresh orange juice

4 Tbsp brown sugar or to taste

1 Tbsp grated orange zest

4 Tbsp coconut butter, melted

Instructions

1. Preheat oven to 360 F/180 C.
2. Place plantain slices in a heatproof dish.
3. Pour the orange juice over plantains, and then sprinkle with brown sugar and grated orange zest.
4. Melt coconut butter and pour evenly over plantains.
5. Cover with foil and bake for 15 to 17 minutes.
6. Serve warm or cold with honey or maple syrup.

Nutrition Facts

Percent daily values based on the Reference Daily Intake (RDI) for a 2000 calorie diet.

Amount Per Serving

Calories 350.51 | Calories From Fat (4%) 14 | Total Fat 1.64g 3% | Saturated Fat 0.83g 4% | Cholesterol 2.15mg <1% | Sodium 13.04mg <1% | Potassium 1139.42mg 33% | Total Carbohydrates 85.34g 28% | Fiber 5.36g 21% | Sugar 46g | Protein 3g 6%

Powerful Peas & Lentils Dip

Ready in Time: 10 minutes | Servings: 4

Ingredients

4 cups frozen peas
2 cup green lentils cooked
1 piece of grated ginger
1/2 cup fresh basil chopped
1 cup ground almonds
Juice of 1/2 lime
Pinch of salt
4 Tbsp sesame oil
1/4 cup Sesame seeds

Instructions

1. Place all ingredients in a food processor or in a blender.
2. Blend until all ingredients combined well.
3. Keep refrigerated in an airtight container up to 4 days.

Nutrition Facts

Percent daily values based on the Reference Daily Intake (RDI) for a 2000 calorie diet.

Amount Per Serving

Calories 561.49 | Calories From Fat (51%) 287.84 | Total Fat 33.64g 52% | Saturated Fat 4g 20% | Cholesterol 0mg 0% | Sodium 149.13mg 6% | Potassium 825.81mg 24% | Total Carbohydrates 47g 16% | Fiber 18.61g 74% | Sugar 9.48g | Protein 23.8g 48%

Protein "Raffaello" Candies

Ready in Time: 15 minutes | Servings: 12

Ingredients

1 1/2 cups desiccated coconut flakes
1/2 cup coconut butter softened
4 Tbsp coconut milk canned
4 Tbs coconut palm sugar (or granulated sugar)
1 tsp pure vanilla extract
1 Tbsp vegan protein powder (pea or soy)
15 whole almonds

Instructions

1. Put 1 cup of desiccated coconut flakes, and all remaining ingredients in the blender (except almonds), and blend until soft.
2. If your dough is too thick, add some coconut milk.
3. In a bowl, add remaining coconut flakes.
4. Coat every almond in one tablespoon of mixture and roll into a ball.
5. Roll each ball in coconut flakes.
6. Chill in the fridge for several hours.

Nutrition Facts

Percent daily values based on the Reference Daily Intake (RDI) for a 2000 calorie diet.

Amount Per Serving

Calories 212.41 | Calories From Fat (81%) 171.5 | Total Fat 20.32g 31% | Saturated Fat 15g 75% | Cholesterol 0.15mg <1% | Sodium 8mg <1% | Potassium 137.36mg 4% | Total Carbohydrates 7.62g 3% | Fiber 2.5g 12% | Sugar 3.29g | Protein 3g 6%

Protein-Rich Pumpkin Bowl

Ready in Time: 10 minutes | Servings: 2

Ingredients

1 1/2 cups almond milk (more or less depending on desired consistency)

1 cup pumpkin puree canned, with salt

1/2 cup chopped walnuts

1 scoop vegan soy protein powder

1 tsp pure vanilla extract

A handful of cacao nibs

Instructions

1. Add all ingredients in a blender apart from the cacao nibs.
2. Blend until smooth.
3. Serve in bowls and sprinkle with cacao nibs.

Nutrition Facts

Percent daily values based on the Reference Daily Intake (RDI) for a 2000 calorie diet.

Amount Per Serving

Calories 396.6 | Calories From Fat (50%) 198.8 | Total Fat 23.38g 36% | Saturated Fat 2.11g 11% | Cholesterol 2.31mg <1% | Sodium 425.59mg 18% | Potassium 840.34mg 24% | Total Carbohydrates 30.7g 10% | Fiber 9.19g 37% | Sugar 13.1g | Protein 19.6g 39%

Savory Red Potato-Garlic Balls

Ready in Time: 40 minutes | Servings: 4

Ingredients

1 1/2 lbs of red potatoes
3 cloves of garlic finely chopped
1 Tbsp of fresh finely chopped parsley
1/4 tsp ground turmeric
Salt and ground pepper to taste

Instructions

1. Rinse potatoes and place unpeeled into a large pot.
2. Pour water to cover potatoes and bring to boil.
3. Cook for about 20 to 25 minutes on medium heat.
4. Rinse potatoes and let them cool down.
5. Peel potatoes and mash them; add finely chopped garlic, and the salt and pepper.
6. Form the potato mixture into small balls.
7. Sprinkle with chopped parsley and refrigerate for several hours.
8. Serve.

Nutrition Facts

Percent daily values based on the Reference Daily Intake (RDI) for a 2000 calorie diet.

Amount Per Serving

Calories 138.56 | Calories From Fat (1%) 1.66 | Total Fat 0.19g <1% | Saturated Fat 0.03g <1% | Cholesterol 0mg 0% | Sodium 156.52mg 7% | Potassium 941.43mg 27% | Total Carbohydrates 31.47g 10% | Fiber 2.83g 11% | Sugar 0.03g | Protein 4g 8%

Spicy Smooth Red Lentil Dip

Ready in Time: 35 minutes | Servings: 4

Ingredients

1 cup red lentils
1 bay leaf
Sea salt to taste
2 garlic clove, finely chopped
2 Tbsp chopped cilantro leaves
1 Tbsp tomato paste
Lemon juice from 2 lemons, freshly squeezed
2 tsp ground cumin
4 Tbsp extra-virgin olive oil

Instructions

1. Rinse lentils and drain.
2. Combine lentils and bay leaf in a medium saucepan.
3. Pour enough water to cover lentils completely, and bring to boil.
4. Cover tightly, reduce heat to medium, and simmer for about 20 minutes.
5. Season salt to taste, and stir well. Note: Always season with the salt after cooking – if salt is added before, the lentils will become tough.
6. Drain the lentils in a colander. Discard the bay leaf and let the lentils cool for 10 minutes.
7. Transfer the lentils to a food processor and add all remaining ingredients.
8. Pulse until all ingredients combined well.
9. Taste and adjust seasonings if needed.
10. Transfer a lentil dip into a glass container and refrigerate at least 2 hours before serving.

Nutrition Facts

Percent daily values based on the Reference Daily Intake (RDI) for a 2000 calorie diet.

Amount Per Serving

Calories 297.66 | Calories From Fat (44%) 130.57 | Total Fat 14.84g 23% | Saturated Fat 2g 10% | Cholesterol 0mg 0% | Sodium 39.41mg 2% | Potassium 368mg 11% | Total Carbohydrates 31g 10% | Fiber 5.6g 22% | Sugar 0.83g | Protein 12.53g 25%

Steamed Broccoli with Sesame

Ready in Time: 15 minutes | Servings: 2

Ingredients

1 1/2 lb fresh broccoli florets
1/2 cup sesame oil
4 Tbsp sesame seeds
Salt and ground pepper to taste

Instruction

1. Place broccoli florets in a steamer basket above boiling water.
2. Cover and steam for about 4 to 5 minutes.
3. Remove from steam and place broccoli in serving the dish.
4. Season with the salt and pepper, and drizzle with sesame oil; toss to coat.
5. Sprinkle with sesame seeds and serve immediately.

Nutrition Facts

Percent daily values based on the Reference Daily Intake (RDI) for a 2000 calorie diet.

Amount Per Serving

Calories 674.38 | Calories From Fat (84%) 565.72 | Total Fat 64.56g 99% | Saturated Fat 9.16g 46% | Cholesterol 0mg 0% | Sodium 233.59mg 10% | Potassium 1122.5mg 32% | Total Carbohydrates 20.6g 7% | Fiber 2.12g 8% | Sugar 0.05g | Protein 13g 26%

Vegan Eggplant Patties

Ready in Time: 30 minutes | Servings: 6

Ingredients

2 big eggplants
1 onion finely diced
1 Tbsp smashed garlic cloves
1 bunch raw parsley, chopped
1/2 cup almond meal
4 Tbsp Kalamata olives, pitted and sliced
1 Tbsp baking soda
Salt and ground pepper to taste
Olive oil or avocado oil, for frying

Instructions

1. Peel off eggplants, rinse, and cut in half.
2. Sauté eggplant cubes in a non-stick skillet - occasionally stirring - about 10 minutes.
3. Transfer to a large bowl and mash with an immersion blender.
4. Add eggplant puree into a bowl and add in all remaining ingredients (except oil).
5. Knead a mixture using your hands until the dough is smooth, sticky, and easy to shape.
6. Shape mixture into 6 patties.
7. Heat the olive oil in a frying skillet on medium-high heat.
8. Fry patties for about 3 to 4 minutes per side.
9. Remove patties on a platter lined with kitchen paper towel to drain.
10. Serve warm.

Nutrition Facts

Percent daily values based on the Reference Daily Intake (RDI) for a 2000 calorie diet.

Amount Per Serving

Calories 156.96 | Calories From Fat (70%) 109.33 | Total Fat 12.43g 19% | Saturated Fat 1.73g 9% | Cholesterol 0mg 0% | Sodium 702.89mg 29% | Potassium 568.29mg 16% | Total Carbohydrates 11.63g 4% | Fiber 6,.68g 27% | Sugar 3.97g | Protein 2.75g 6%

SWEETS/DESSERTS

Beets Bars with Dry Fruits

Ready in Time: 55 minutes | Servings: 6

Ingredients

1 Tbsp flax seed
3 Tbsp water
5 oz whole wheat flour
8 ounces beetroot, boiled and mashed
3 Tbsp chopped dates
3 Tbsp chopped figs
4 Tbsp honey (preferably a darker honey)
4 Tbsp olive oil
1 tsp baking powder
1 tsp baking soda
1 tsp pure vanilla extract
1/4 tsp salt

Instructions

1. Preheat oven to 300F.
2. Soak the flaxseed with water for 10 minutes.
3. Grease a baking sheet with olive oil; set aside.
4. Place the wheat flour along with all remaining ingredients into a food processor.
5. Process until all ingredients are combined well.
6. Place the mixture into the prepared baking sheet and bake for 35 to 40 minutes.
7. Remove the baking sheet from the oven, and let it cool completely.
8. Cut into squares and serve.
9. Store into a container and refrigerate up to 4 days.

Nutrition Facts

Percent daily values based on the Reference Daily Intake (RDI) for a 2000 calorie diet.

Amount Per Serving

Calories 247.79 | Calories From Fat (41%) 102.12 | Total Fat 11.57g 18% | Saturated Fat 1.5g 8% | Cholesterol 0mg 0% | Sodium 220mg 9% | Potassium 159.18mg 5% | Total Carbohydrates 33.91g 11% | Fiber 1.8g 7% | Sugar 14.64g | Protein 3.1g 6%

Cocoa, Avocado and Chia Cream

Ready in Time: 15 minutes | Servings: 4

Ingredients

3 Tbsp cocoa powder, dry unsweetened

2 ripe avocados peeled and cut into cubes

3 Tbsp coconut oil melted

3/4 cup honey strained

1 tsp ground chia seeds

1 tsp pure vanilla extract

Serving: chopped nuts (optional)

Instructions

1. Combine all ingredients in a high-speed blender and blend until smooth and well combined.
2. Divide mixture among cups and refrigerate for at least 2 hours before serving
3. Sprinkle with chopped nuts and serve.

Nutrition Facts

Percent daily values based on the Reference Daily Intake (RDI) for a 2000 calorie diet.

Amount Per Serving

Calories 503.84 | Calories From Fat (50%) 250.86 | Total Fat 29.63g 46% | Saturated Fat 11.71g 59% | Cholesterol 0mg 0% | Sodium 13.4mg <1% | Potassium 685.38mg 20% | Total Carbohydrates 66.3g 22% | Fiber 10.71g 43% | Sugar 52.75g | Protein 3.82g 8%

Coconut Balls with Lemon Rinds

Ready in Time: 15 minutes | Servings: 8

Ingredients

1 cup coconut butter softened

1 cup coconut milk canned

1 cup coconut shreds

1/2 cup ground almonds (without salt)

1/2 tsp cinnamon

1 tsp pure vanilla extract

1/2 tsp nutmeg

2 Tbsp honey or maple syrup

Coating and serving

1 cup Coconut shreds for coating

2 lemon zest (finely grated fresh)

Instructions

1. Add all ingredients into the food processor; process until creamy.
2. Pour the mixture in a refrigerator for 2 hours.
3. Form the mixture into balls, and roll them in coconut shreds.
4. Arrange balls on a plate, sprinkle with lemon rinds and refrigerate until firm.
5. Serve.

Nutrition Facts

Percent daily values based on the Reference Daily Intake (RDI) for a 2000 calorie diet.

Amount Per Serving

Calories 427.96 | Calories From Fat (83%) 355 | Total Fat 41.27g 63% | Saturated Fat 27.12g 136% | Cholesterol 61mg 20% | Sodium 39.8mg 2% | Potassium 218.48mg 6% | Total Carbohydrates 15.3g 5% | Fiber 2.57g 10% | Sugar 10.54g | Protein 3.25g 7%

Coconut Rice Pudding with Cardamom

Ready in Time: 35 minutes | Servings: 6

Ingredients

9 oz Arborio or other short-grain rice
2 1/4 cups water
2 1/4 cups coconut milk canned
1 1/2 cups coconut butter melted
1 cup granulated sugar
1/4 tsp ground cardamom
1 tsp cinnamon seeds
Cinnamon, powder, for serving

Instructions

1. Add rice, water, coconut milk and coconut butter in a saucepan, and bring to boil.
2. Add sugar, cardamom, and cinnamon seeds; give a good stir.
3. Reduce the heat to medium-low and simmer for 20-25 minutes, stirring constantly.
4. Once the rice has started to thicken, remove the saucepan from heat, cover, and let it rest for 5 minutes.
5. Sprinkle with cinnamon on top and serve warm or cold.
6. Keep refrigerated.

Nutrition Facts

Percent daily values based on the Reference Daily Intake (RDI) for a 2000 calorie diet.

Amount Per Serving

Calories 629.3 | Calories From Fat (49%) 310.67 | Total Fat 37.11g 57% | Saturated Fat 32.75g 164% | Cholesterol 0mg 0% | Sodium 18.12mg <1% | Potassium 395.3mg 11% | Total Carbohydrates 73.52g 25% | Fiber 2,51g 10% | Sugar 33,27g | Protein 6,55g 13%

Coconutty Cake

Ready in Time: 25 minutes | Servings: 4

Ingredients

1/2 lb coconut butter melted
3/4 cup granulated sugar
1/4 lb of ground walnuts
1/2 cup coconut flour
2 Tbsp cornflour
1 Tbsp arrowroot powder
1 tsp baking powder

Instructions

1. Preheat your oven to 360 F/180 C.
2. Add all ingredients into a food processor.
3. Process until combined well and get a uniform texture.
4. Pour the mixture in a large mold and place it in the oven.
5. Bake for about 12 to 15 minutes.
6. Let sit for 10 minutes, remove from mold, and serve.

Nutrition Facts

Percent daily values based on the Reference Daily Intake (RDI) for a 2000 calorie diet.

Amount Per Serving

Calories 538.39 | Calories From Fat (60%) 320.41 | Total Fat 38,.29g 59% | Saturated Fat 19.19g 96% | Cholesterol 0mg 0% | Sodium 125.33mg 5% | Potassium 319.86mg 9% | Total Carbohydrates 49.5g 17% | Fiber 3.45g 14% | Sugar 38.22g | Protein 6.71g 13%

Dark Honey Hazelnut Cookies

Ready in Time: 30 minutes | Servings: 12

Ingredients

1 Tbsp olive oil
1/2 cup ground hazelnuts
1/2 tsp baking soda
1 1/2 cups of hazelnut flour
2 Tbsp of coconut flour
1/2 tsp cinnamon
Pinch of salt
1 medium banana mashed
2 Tbsp coconut oil melted
4 Tbsp dark honey strained
1 tsp of pure vanilla extract

Instructions

1. Preheat oven to 340 F.
2. Grease a baking sheet with olive oil; set aside.
3. Combine together ground hazelnuts, baking soda, hazelnut flour, coconut flour, cinnamon, and salt in a bowl.
4. In a separate bowl, whisk mashed banana, coconut oil, dark honey, and vanilla extract.
5. Combine the hazelnut flour mixture with the egg mixture; beat with the electric mixer until smooth and combined well.
6. Shape the dough into 12 balls; place in a prepared baking sheet.
7. Bake for about 17 to 18 minutes.
8. Remove from the oven; leave to cool for 15 minutes and serve.
9. Keep stored in a covered container.

Nutrition Facts

Percent daily values based on the Reference Daily Intake (RDI) for a 2000 calorie diet.

Amount Per Serving

Calories 99.65 | Calories From Fat (56%) 55.45 | Total Fat 6.5g 10% | Saturated Fat 2.36g 12% | Cholesterol 0mg 0% | Sodium 508.6mg 21% | Potassium 78.48mg 2% | Total Carbohydrates 10.15g 3% | Fiber 1g 4% | Sugar 7.13g | Protein 1.8g 4%

Energy Dried Figs Brownies

Ready in Time: 15 minutes | Servings: 4

Ingredients

1 cup dried figs finely chopped
2 Tbsp cocoa powder
1 cup almonds chopped
2 Tbsp extracted honey
1 scoop protein powder (pea or soy)
2 Tbsp of water

Instructions

1. Add all ingredients in a food processor.
2. Process until combined well.
3. Transfer mixture into a bowl, and knead with your hands.
4. Lay a mixture on working surface and roll dough into about 1/3 of an inch thick sheet.
5. Cut the mixture into the square.
6. Refrigerate for one hour before serving.

Nutrition Facts

Percent daily values based on the Reference Daily Intake (RDI) for a 2000 calorie diet.

Amount Per Serving

Calories 347.41 | Calories From Fat (46%) 160.54 | Total Fat 19.14g 29% | Saturated Fat 1.7g 9% | Cholesterol 0.58mg <1% | Sodium 15mg <1% | Potassium 576.7mg 16% | Total Carbohydrates 41.83g 14% | Fiber 8.52g 34% | Sugar 28.38g | Protein 10.31g 21%

Hearty Apple Bran Muffins

Ready in Time: 30 minutes | Servings: 12

Ingredients

1 cup all-purpose flour
1/3 cup brown sugar (packed)
2 tsp baking powder
1/4 tsp salt
1/4 tsp ground cinnamon
1/4 tsp ground nutmeg
1 cup tart apple peeled, finely chopped
3/4 cup water
1/2 cup soy milk
1/4 cup canola oil (or other vegan low saturated fat oil)
1/2 mashed banana
2 cups bran flake cereal

Instructions

1. Preheat oven to 400 F.
2. Grease with oil 12 muffin cups; set aside.
3. In a bowl, combine together flour, brown sugar, baking powder, salt, cinnamon, and nutmeg.
4. In a separate bowl, whisk together apple, water, dry milk, vegetable oil and egg in small bowl; add to flour mixture and stir until moistened.
5. Finely, add in bran cereals and stir well.
6. Spoon mixture into prepared muffin cups, filling 2/3 full.
7. Bake for 12 to 15 minutes.
8. Your muffins are ready when wooden pick inserted in the center comes out clean.
9. Remove muffins to a wire rack and cool slightly.
10. Store muffins in an airtight container up to 4 days.

Nutrition Facts

Percent daily values based on the Reference Daily Intake (RDI) for a 2000 calorie diet.

Amount Per Serving

Calories 137.6 | Calories From Fat (32%) 44.38 | Total Fat 5g 8% | Saturated Fat 0.44g 2% | Cholesterol 0mg 0% | Sodium 186.17mg 8% | Potassium 96.71mg 3% | Total Carbohydrates 22.4g 7% | Fiber 1.81g 7% | Sugar 9.11g | Protein 2.12g 4%

Honey Raisins Crispy Balls

Ready in Time: 15 minutes | Servings: 15

Ingredients

1/2 cup powdered sugar
1/2 cup honey
1/2 cup peanut butter
1-1/2 cups crispy rice cereal
1/2 cup raisins

Instructions

1. Place a sheet of waxed paper on a cookie sheet.
2. Combine together sugar, honey, and peanut butter in a medium bowl.
3. Stir until mixed well. Stir in cereal and raisins.
4. Shape the mixture into 1-inch balls.
5. Refrigerate for 2 hours or until firm.
6. Keep stored in a tightly covered container in the refrigerator.

Nutrition Facts

Percent daily values based on the Reference Daily Intake (RDI) for a 2000 calorie diet.

Amount Per Serving

Calories 55.94 | Calories From Fat (33%) 18.38 | Total Fat 2.2g 3% | Saturated Fat 0.46g 2% | Cholesterol 0mg 0% | Sodium 30.95mg 1% | Potassium 52.8mg 2% | Total Carbohydrates 8.92g 3% | Fiber 0.38g 2% | Sugar 6.81g | Protein 1.27g 3%

Protein Banana and Vanilla Cream

Ready in Time: 10 minutes | Servings: 2

Ingredients

1 cup almond milk
2 ripe bananas peeled and thinly sliced
2 Tbsp almond butter (plain, unsalted)
1 Tbsp pure vanilla extract
2 Tbsp granulated sugar (or to taste)
1 scoop vegan protein powder (e.g., chia, soy or hemp)

Instructions

1. Add all ingredients into a high-speed blender.
2. Blend until smooth and creamy.
3. If the cream is too thick, add some more almond milk.
4. Pour mixture into glass jar or container and chill for 2 hours.
5. Serve! Enjoy!

Nutrition Facts

Percent daily values based on the Reference Daily Intake (RDI) for a 2000 calorie diet.

Amount Per Serving

Calories 327.56 | Calories From Fat (32%) 104.45 | Total Fat 12.32g 19% | Saturated Fat 1.4g 7% | Cholesterol 0mg 0% | Sodium 26.9mg 1% | Potassium 673.73mg 19% | Total Carbohydrates 50.1g 17% | Fiber 5.18g 21% | Sugar 34.15g | Protein 5.14g 10%

Protein Carrot Macaroons

Ready in Time: 45 minutes | Servings: 8

Ingredients

2 large carrots grated

1/4 cup water

1/2 cup sesame oil

2 cups coconut flakes

1 Tbsp protein powder (brown rice or chia)

3/4 cup rice flour

Pinch of salt

1 tsp pure vanilla extract

3 Tbsp agave syrup

Instructions

1. Preheat oven to 350 F/175 C.
2. Grease a baking sheet with sesame oil; set aside.
3. Knead all ingredients together in a large bowl until well combined.
4. Shape the mixture into balls.
5. Arrange balls on a prepared baking sheet and bake for 30 minutes, rotating once.
6. Remove the macaroons from the pan and allow them to cool completely.

Nutrition Facts

Percent daily values based on the Reference Daily Intake (RDI) for a 2000 calorie diet.

Amount Per Serving

Calories 289.15 | Calories From Fat (64%) 184.58 | Total Fat 21.25g 33% | Saturated Fat 8g 40% | Cholesterol 0.58mg <1% | Sodium 27.24mg 1% | Potassium 207.6mg 6% | Total Carbohydrates 23.16g 8% | Fiber 3.2g 13% | Sugar 8.92g | Protein 3.19g 6%

Raw Lemon 'Cheesecake'

Ready in Time: 6 hours and 15 minutes | Servings: 10

Ingredients

For the crust
2 cups raw almonds ground
2 Tbsp coconut flakes
1/4 tsp vanilla extract
1/4 cup date paste
1/4 tsp sea salt
For the filling
3/4 cup coconut oil, melted
1 cup Lemon juice (freshly squeezed)
1 cup almond milk
1 1/2 cups ground nuts (almonds, peanuts)
3/4 cup extracted honey
1 tsp vanilla extract

Instructions

1. Add all ingredients for the crust into your food processor or high-speed blender.
2. Blend/process until smooth and combined well.
3. Pour the mixture into the round pan and refrigerate for 2 hours.
4. Combine all ingredients for filling into a blender and beat about 30 to 45 seconds.
5. Pour the mixture evenly over the cake crust.
6. Freeze cheesecake for 4 hours.
7. Serve and enjoy!

Nutrition Facts

Percent daily values based on the Reference Daily Intake (RDI) for a 2000 calorie diet.

Amount Per Serving

Calories 414.21 | Calories From Fat (65%) 270.91 | Total Fat 31.2g 49% | Saturated Fat 14.56g 73% | Cholesterol 0.8mg <1% | Sodium 561.13mg 23% | Potassium 409.17mg 12% | Total Carbohydrates 29.12g 10% | Fiber 5.86g 23% | Sugar 18.13g | Protein 8.42g 17%

Semolina Cake with Brown Sugar Syrup

Ready in Time: 1 hour and 30 minutes | Servings: 14

Ingredients

1 Tbsp olive oil or non-stick cooking spray
For cake:
1 1/2 cup fine semolina
1 1/2 cup coarse semolina
1 1/2 cup sugar
2 1/2 cups coconut milk (canned)
2 tsp of baking powder
1 tsp pure vanilla extract
For syrup:
1 1/2 cup water
2 1/2 cup brown sugar (packed)

Instructions

1. Preheat oven to 360 F.
2. Grease a baking dish with oil or cooking spray; set aside.
3. Combine all ingredients for the cake in a mixing bowl; beat with an electric mixer until combined well.
4. Pour the batter in a prepared baking dish.
5. Bake for 1 hour and 15 minutes.
6. Remove the cake from the oven and cut diagonally with a warm knife.
7. In a saucepan, cook water and sugar over medium heat for about 6 minutes or until sugar is completely dissolved (for thick syrup).
8. Pour hot syrup evenly over the cake.
9. Let cool on room temperature and serve.

Nutrition Facts

Percent daily values based on the Reference Daily Intake (RDI) for a 2000 calorie diet.

Amount Per Serving

Calories 410.53 | Calories From Fat (12%) 47.7 | Total Fat 5.64g 9% | Saturated Fat 4g 20% | Cholesterol 0mg 0% | Sodium 84.6mg 4% | Potassium 164.47mg 5% | Total Carbohydrates 86.81g 29% | Fiber 1.4g 6% | Sugar 59.54g | Protein 5g 10%

Strawberries, Quinoa and Silk Tofu Dessert

Preparation Time: 35 minutes | Servings: 3

Ingredients

1 cup strawberries halved

4 Tbsp brown sugar - (packed)

1/2 cup cooked quinoa

1 cup silken tofu mashed

1 fresh juice of half a lemon

1/2 tsp pure vanilla extract

Instructions

1. Add strawberries and sugar in a bowl, cover and set aside for half an hour.
2. In the meantime, cook quinoa in one cup of water for about 15 to 20 minutes or until water is absorbed.
3. Remove from the heat, uncover and mash with a fork.
4. Place strawberries, quinoa, and all remaining ingredients into a blender and blend until combined well without lumps.
5. Taste and adjust sugar to taste.
6. Refrigerate mixture for one hour before serving.

Nutrition Facts

Percent daily values based on the Reference Daily Intake (RDI) for a 2000 calorie diet.

Amount Per Serving

Calories 233.17 | Calories From Fat (14%) 33.2 | Total Fat 3.72g 6% | Saturated Fat 0,45g 2% | Cholesterol 0mg 0% | Sodium 10.5mg <1% | Potassium 402.76mg 12% | Total Carbohydrates 43.3g 14% | Fiber 3.12g 12% | Sugar 21.72g | Protein 8g 16%

Strawberry and Banana Ice Cream

Ready in Time: 4 hours and 20 minutes | Servings: 8

Ingredients

2 large frozen bananas
3 cups chopped strawberries
2 1/2 cups coconut milk
1 cup granulated sugar
2 tsp strawberry extract

Instructions

1. Put all ingredients in a blender and blend until soft.
2. Place the mixture in a freezer-safe container and freeze for at least 4 hours or overnight.
3. Transfer frozen mixture to a bowl and beat with a mixer until smooth to break up the ice crystals; repeat the process at least 4 times.
4. Let the ice cream at room temperature for 15 minutes before serving.

Nutrition Facts

Percent daily values based on the Reference Daily Intake (RDI) for a 2000 calorie diet.

Amount Per Serving

Calories 220 | Calories From Fat (31%) 67.4 | Total Fat 8.7g 12% | Saturated Fat 6.6g 35% | Cholesterol 0mg 0% | Sodium 5.71mg <1% | Potassium 281.7mg 8% | Total Carbohydrates 38.34g 13% | Fiber 1.91g 8% | Sugar 31.48g | Protein 1.8g 4%

Sunrise Peach Marmalade

Servings: 4

Ingredients

4 cups fresh peaches diced
1/2 cup peach juice
1 Tbsp finely grated orange peel
3 Tbsp honey extracted
1 Tbsp lemon juice

Instructions

1. Place all ingredients in a blender or food processor; blend until combined well.
2. Pour mixture into a glass microwave-safe dish.
3. Uncovered, microwave on HIGH for 15 to 17 minutes, stirring every 5 minutes.
4. Allow it to cool.
5. Serve with crusty bread, ice cream, fruits...etc.
6. Keep refrigerated.

Nutrition Facts

Percent daily values based on the Reference Daily Intake (RDI) for a 2000 calorie diet.

Amount Per Serving

Calories 130.22 | Calories From Fat (3%) 3.69 | Total Fat 0.5g <1% | Saturated Fat 0,04g <1% | Cholesterol 0mg 0% | Sodium 2mg <1% | Potassium 378.3mg 11% | Total Carbohydrates 33.5g 11% | Fiber 3.16g 13% | Sugar 30.5g | Protein 2g 4%

Vegan Blueberry Ice Cream

Preparation Time: 20 minutes | Servings: 8

Ingredients

4 cups fresh blueberries (or frozen blueberries)
1 1/2 cups granulated sugar
2 Tbsp water
1 Tbsp arrowroot powder
2 cups coconut cream softened

Instructions

1. Add blueberries, sugar, and water in a saucepan.
2. Cook, frequently stirring, over medium heat; bring to a boil.
3. Reduce heat to low and stir for about 10 minutes over low heat or until blueberries are softened,
4. Strain the mixture, and discard seeds and skins.
5. Add the coconut cream and beat with an electric mixer until soft and creamy.
6. Pour the mixture in a freezer-safe container and freeze for 4 to 5 hours.
7. Transfer frozen mixture to a bowl and beat with a mixer until smooth to avoid ice cream crystallization.
8. Repeat this process at least 4 times.
9. Remove from the freezer 15 minutes before servings.

Nutrition Facts

Percent daily values based on the Reference Daily Intake (RDI) for a 2000 calorie diet.

Amount Per Serving

Calories 242.9 | Calories From Fat (70%) 170.2 | Total Fat 21.05g 32% | Saturated Fat 18.47g 92% | Cholesterol 0mg 0% | Sodium 3.26mg <1% | Potassium 250.7mg 7% | Total Carbohydrates 17.25g 6% | Fiber 3g 12% | Sugar 7.22g | Protein 2.72g 5%

Vegan Hazelnut - Coffee Truffles

Preparation Time: 25 minutes | Servings: 12

Ingredients

Base:

1 1/2 cups hazelnuts (soaked)

1/4 cup water

1/4 cup maple syrup

Pinch of sea salt

2 tsp vanilla seeds

1 Tbsp coffee extract

1/4 cup coconut oil softened

Glaze:

1/2 cup coconut oil softened

1/2 cup cacao powder

1/4 cup maple syrup

a pinch of salt

Instructions

1. Add all base ingredients into a food processor; process until smooth and well incorporated.
2. Pour mixture into a bowl and place in the freezer until firm.
3. Shape mixture into balls (about 12).
4. Place on foil and place back in the freezer to harden.
5. To make a glaze: whisk together all glaze ingredients until smooth.
6. Dip balls into the glaze mixture and place them on the foil.
7. Place them back in the freezer to set completely.

Nutrition Facts

Percent daily values based on the Reference Daily Intake (RDI) for a 2000 calorie diet.

Amount Per Serving

Calories 297.45 | Calories From Fat (77%) 230.4 | Total Fat 27.12g 42% | Saturated Fat 13g 65% | Cholesterol 0mg 0% | Sodium 2.57mg <1% | Potassium 241.38mg 7% | Total Carbohydrates 14.68g 5% | Fiber 3.15g 13% | Sugar 9.15g | Protein 3.84g 8%

Vegan Protein - Chocolate Ice Cream

Preparation Time: 20 minutes | Servings: 5

Ingredients

1 can (15 oz) coconut milk, unsweetened
1 Tbsp cornflour
1/4 cup cacao powder, unsweetened
1/4 cup maple syrup
1 tsp vanilla extract
2 scoop protein powder (pea or soy)
For serving/garnish - chopped walnuts and golden raisins

Instructions

1. Combine together all ingredients into a high-speed blender and blend until creamy and smooth.
2. Transfer the mixture in a freezer-safe container and freeze until firm (not less than 4 hours).
3. Transfer frozen mixture to a bowl and beat with a mixer to break up the ice crystals. Repeat this process at least 4 times.
4. Let the ice cream at room temperature for 15 minutes before serving.

Nutrition Facts

Percent daily values based on the Reference Daily Intake (RDI) for a 2000 calorie diet.

Amount Per Serving

Calories 358.78 | Calories From Fat (72%) 259.5 | Total Fat 31g 48% | Saturated Fat 17.59g 88% | Cholesterol 0.92mg <1% | Sodium 28.2mg 1% | Potassium 418mg 12% | Total Carbohydrates 19.85g 7% | Fiber 3g 12% | Sugar 10.43g | Protein 8g 16%

Winter Pumpkin Pancakes

Ready in Time: 30 minutes | Servings: 6

Ingredients

2 cups all-purpose flour
2 Tbsp brown sugar - (packed)
1 Tbsp baking powder
1 1/4 tsp pumpkin pie spice
Pinch or two of salt
1 3/4 cups almond milk
1/2 cup pure pumpkin (canned)
1 Tbsp silken tofu mashed
2 Tbsp sesame oil
Serving
Honey
Chopped nuts (optional)

Instructions

1. In a large bowl, combine together flour, brown sugar, baking powder, pumpkin pie spice, and salt.
2. In a separate bowl, stir almond milk, pumpkin, silken tofu, and sesame oil.
3. Add almond milk mixture to the flour mixture; stir just until moistened.
4. Heat griddle or skillet over medium heat; brush lightly with vegetable oil.
5. Pour 1/4 cup batter onto hot griddle; cook until bubbles begin to burst.
6. Turn and continue cooking 1 to 2 minutes. Repeat with the remaining batter.
7. Serve with hot with honey and chopped nuts.

Nutrition Facts

Percent daily values based on the Reference Daily Intake (RDI) for a 2000 calorie diet.

Amount Per Serving

Calories 295.39 | Calories From Fat (36%) 105.84 | Total Fat 12.33g 19% | Saturated Fat 1.32g 7% | Cholesterol 31mg 10% | Sodium 694.91mg 29% | Potassium 150.12mg 4% | Total Carbohydrates 40.22g 13% | Fiber 2.43g 10% | Sugar 5.45g | Protein 7.7g 16%

One Last Thing...

DID YOU ENJOY THE BOOK?

IF SO, THEN LET ME KNOW BY LEAVING A REVIEW ON AMAZON! Reviews are the lifeblood of independent authors. I would appreciate even a few words and rating if that's all you have time for

IF YOU DID NOT LIKE THIS BOOK, THEN PLEASE TELL ME! Email me at perfectecruz@gmail.com and let me know what you didn't like! Perhaps I can change it. In today's world, a book doesn't have to be stagnant; it can improve with time and feedback from readers like you. You can impact this book, and I welcome your feedback. Help make this book better for everyone!

VEGAN MEAL PREP COOKBOOK FOR ATHLETES

100 HIGH PROTEIN, WHOLE FOOD, PLANT BASED RECIPES TO BUILD MUSCLES AND IMPROVE YOUR HEALTH

Joseph P. Turner

MEAL PREP

Planning and preparing your meals ahead of time will make healthy choices an easy task, and it will link you with good dietary habits.

Having pre-prepared meals on hand can also choose a portion size and help you reach your nutrition goals.

Some researches found that one of the biggest barriers athletes report in their journey towards healthier eating is not having enough time in the day to cook or prepare meals.

Athletes have tight schedules, where they might be eating meals at strange hours, and sometimes get so busy that they are relying on bars and shakes for too many meals.

Follow these meal prep tips:

- ✓ Write a Shopping list of all the ingredients you will need to buy to make the meals in your weekly plan. To have all in one place, we recommend downloading some shopping list applications or to create a shopping list with your Google Assistant on Google Home.
- ✓ Purchase the right containers, all kinds, and different shapes. The best choice is to purchase a glass or ceramic vessel refractory containers with locking lids. The best types of packaging for the freezer:
  - Ziploc Freezer Bags
  - Vacuum Sealer
  - Tupperware freezer containers

- ✓ Organize your time for cooking. If you are a busy person, seizure your weekend to get your meal prepping done, so you've got meals for the beginning of the week.
- ✓ Check grocery stores in your beforehand. Use Internet research for online grocery shopping; it saves your time and money.
- ✓ Use healthy cooking methods such as baking, steaming, broiling, grilling, and roasting.
- ✓ Instant Pot meal prep can make the week ahead a lot easier to deal with it.

Important Note: According to the Food and Drug Administration, after food is cooked, it should sit out at room temperature no more than two hours before being refrigerated or frozen!

How to properly reheat your refrigerated/frozen food?

- Reheat sauces, soups, and gravies by bringing them to a rolling boil.
- Cover your food to reheat; this retains moisture.
- Put any foods that don't have much or any sauce (potatoes, steamed veggies) in stainless steel or cast-iron pan; reheat over medium-high heat.
- Pour the soup/stew into a microwave-safe container and heat the soup/stew on high for 20 to 30 seconds.
- **Do not reheat in the microwave oven**: Leafy greens, Chili peppers, fruits, Red pasta sauce, bread, Anything reheated before.

BREAKFAST

Almond Queen Fruit Smoothie

Ready in Time: 10 minutes | Servings: 2

Ingredients

1 1/2 cup almond milk

1 small peeled banana cut into 1-inch chunks and frozen

1 cup frozen peaches, sliced, thawed

3 Tbsp toasted almonds ground

1 scoop protein powder (pea or soy)

1 Tbsp flaxseed (ground)

Instructions

1. Add all ingredients into a high-speed blender and blend until smooth.

2. Pour your smoothie into the bottle, glass, or Mason jars; cover and keep refrigerated up to 2 days.

3. Or, pour your smoothie into a freezer-safe Ziploc bag and freeze up to 3 months.

4. Let it defrost in the refrigerator overnight, stir and enjoy!

Nutrition Facts

Percent daily values based on the Reference Daily Intake (RDI) for a 2000 calorie diet.

Amount Per Serving

Calories 262 | Calories From Fat (26%) 67.61 | Total Fat 8g 12% |

Saturated Fat 0.7g 3% | Cholesterol 1.16mg <1% | Sodium 26.49mg 1% | Potassium 497.5mg 14% | Total Carbohydrates 45.27g 15% |

Fiber 5.6g 21% | Sugar 34.85g | Protein 6.58g 13%

Baked Raisins & Pumpkin Energy Bars

Ready in time: 35 minutes | Servings: 8

Ingredients

1 Tbsp olive oil for greasing

1 tsp pure vanilla extract

1/2 cup of applesauce

1 1/2 cups of rolled oats

2/3 cup golden raisins

1/2 cup of toasted hazelnuts, chopped

1/2 cup of pumpkin seeds

2 tsp vegan protein powder (e.g., chia, soy or hemp)

1/4 tsp cinnamon

1/2 tsp ginger

Pinch of salt to taste

Instructions

1. Preheat the oven to 350 F.
2. Grease a square baking dish.
3. Stir the vanilla extract and applesauce in a large.
4. Stir the oats into the applesauce mixture.
5. Add all remaining ingredients and stir until thoroughly combined.
6. Spoon mixture into the prepared baking dish and press down until even.
7. Place into oven and bake for about 25 minutes.
8. Remove from the oven, and allow it to cool down completely.
9. Slice into 16 small (or eight large) square or rectangle bars.
10. Wrap each bar with the paper and store at room temperature for up to 3 weeks.
11. Also, you can freeze your energy bars in airtight container or freezer bag to keep it fresh for longer.

Nutrition Facts

Percent daily values based on the Reference Daily Intake (RDI) for a 2000 calorie diet.

Amount Per Serving

Calories 279.13 | Calories From Fat (39%) 109.62 | % Daily Value | Total Fat 12.3g 20% | Saturated Fat 1.24g 6% | Cholesterol 0.19mg <1% | Sodium 303.7mg 13% | Potassium 318.72mg 9% | Total Carbohydrates 38.1g 13% | Fiber 4.16g 17% | Sugar 16.48g | Protein 6g 11%

Baked Savory Oat-Apple Bars

Ready in Time: 45 minutes | Servings: 8

Ingredients

1 Tbs sesame oil (or olive oil)
2 tart apples grated
1/2 cup Instant oats
1/2 cup of Rolled oats
1 cup oat flour
1/4 tsp salt
1 tsp baking powder
3/4 cup of dates
2/3 cup sesame butter or tahini
3 Tbsp Chia seeds
1/2 cup of almond milk
1 tsp pure vanilla extract

Instructions

1. Preheat oven to 350 F.
2. Grease a 9×9" baking pan with oil.
3. Peel and grate apples; place in a colander to drain.
4. In a large bowl, combine Instant and Rolled oats, oat flour, salt, and baking powder.
5. In a separate bowl, stir drained apple, dates, sesame butter, Chia seeds, almond milk, and vanilla extract until everything is combined well (use a mixer).
6. Add apple mixture to the oat mixture and stir until all ingredients are well incorporated
7. Place the batter into a prepared baking pan.
8. Place in the oven, and bake for 30 minutes.
9. Remove pan from the oven, and let cool completely before slicing.
10. Store bars in a sealed container at room temperature for up to 4 days or refrigerate up to one week.

Nutrition Facts

Percent daily values based on the Reference Daily Intake (RDI) for a 2000 calorie diet.

Amount Per Serving

Calories 316 | Calories From Fat (41%) 130.2 | Total Fat 15.8g 24% | Saturated Fat 2.1g 11% | Cholesterol 0mg 0% | Sodium 208mg 9% | Potassium 353.85mg 10% | Total Carbohydrates 41.74g 14% | Fiber 7.16g 29% | Sugar 16g | Protein 7.62g 15%

Boosting Celery-Coconut Smoothie

Ready in Time: 10 minutes | Servings: 2

Ingredients

2 celery stalks, chopped

3 cup kale leaves, fresh and chopped

1 large banana cut into slices

1 1/2 cup coconut milk (canned)

1 Tbsp protein powder (pea or soy)

1 Tbsp lemon juice

1 Tbsp chia seeds

Instructions

1. Add all ingredients in your blender and blend until smooth.

2. Pour your smoothie into the bottle, glass, or Mason jars; cover and keep refrigerated up to 2 days.

3. Or, pour your smoothie into a freezer-safe Ziploc bag and freeze up to 3 months.

4. Let it defrost in the refrigerator overnight, stir and enjoy!

Nutrition Facts

Percent daily values based on the Reference Daily Intake (RDI) for a 2000 calorie diet.

Amount Per Serving

Calories 473.21 | Calories From Fat (70%) 333.57 | Total Fat 39.7g 61% | Saturated Fat 32.49g 162% | Cholesterol 1.16mg <1% | Sodium 89mg 4% | Potassium 926.64mg 26% | Total Carbohydrates 28.8g 10% | Fiber 6.1g 24% | Sugar 9.5g | Protein 9.2g 18%

Breakfast Potato Patties

Ready in Time: 45 minutes Servings: 8

Ingredients

1 1/2 lb grated potatoes

1 grated onion

3 Tbsp applesauce unsweetened (canned)

Salt and ground black pepper to taste

2 Tbsp all-purpose flour

1/2 cup olive or canola oil for frying

Instructions

1. Add all ingredients In a large bowl, and stir until all ingredients combined well.

2. Form the batter into flat patties.

3. Heat oil in a large frying skillet over medium heat.

4. Fry your potato patties for about 6 to 7 minutes, and then flip with a spatula and fry from the other side until done.

5. Remove ready patties on a plate lined with kitchen paper to drain, and completely cool.

6. Transfer your patties in a single layer to baking sheets.

7. Freeze patties until hard.

8. Transfer the frozen patties to freezer bags and keep in freeze up to 2 weeks.

9. Reheat in a microwave oven.

Nutrition Facts

Percent daily values based on the Reference Daily Intake (RDI) for a 2000 calorie diet.

Amount Per Serving

Calories 201.55 | Calories From Fat (60%) 121.42 | Total Fat 13.74g 21% | Saturated Fat 1g 5% | Cholesterol 0mg 0% | Sodium 5.87mg <1% | Potassium 386.69mg 11% | Total Carbohydrates 18.2g 6% | Fiber 2.25g 9% | Sugar 1.5g | Protein 2.8g 6%

Carrot 'Cake' Smoothie

Ready in Time: 10 minutes | Servings: 2

Ingredients

2 grated carrots

2 cups almond milk

4 Tbs rolled oats

1 orange, juiced (about 1/2 cup)

1 Tbsp chia seeds

3/4 tsp cinnamon

1 Tbsp protein powder (pea or soy)

1/2 tsp vanilla extract

Instructions

1. Add all the ingredients to your high-speed blender and blend on high until completely smooth.

2. If your smoothie is too thick, add some more almond milk.

3. Pour your smoothie into the bottle, glass, or Mason jars; cover and keep refrigerated up to 2 days.

4. Or, pour your smoothie into a freezer-safe Ziploc bag and freeze up to 3 months.

5. Let it defrost in the refrigerator overnight, stir and enjoy!

Nutrition Facts

Percent daily values based on the Reference Daily Intake (RDI) for a 2000 calorie diet.

Amount Per Serving

Calories 191.11 | Calories From Fat (21%) 40.41 | Total Fat 4.6g 7% | Saturated Fat 0.59g 3% | Cholesterol 1.16mg <1% | Sodium 76.26mg 3% | Potassium 507.62mg 15% | Total Carbohydrates 30.18g 10% | Fiber 8g 32% | Sugar 7.1g | Protein 8.41g 16%

Carrot, Almond and Dill Muffins

Ready in Time: 45 minutes | Servings: 12

Ingredients

2 cups of pastry flour
2 tsp baking powder
4 Tbsp almond meal
2 Tbsp brown sugar
Pinch of salt
2 tsp fresh dill, finely chopped
1 small ripe banana mashed
1 cup of carrots, grated
3 cup almond milk
1 cup olive oil
1/4 cup apple-sauce unsweetened
2 Tbsp extracted honey

Instructions

1. Preheat oven to 375 F.
2. Grease 12 muffin cups; set aside.
3. Combine pastry flour with the baking powder, almond meal, sugar, carrot, banana, dill, and salt.
4. In a separate bowl, beat the almond milk, applesauce, and honey with a hand mixer.
5. Slowly, add the milk mixture to the flour mixture and beat until combined well.
6. Divide the mixture into the prepared muffin cups (3/4 of a cup).
7. Bake for about 30 to 35 minutes or until a toothpick inserted inside comes out clean.
8. Remove from the oven, and allow to cool completely,
9. Store your muffins in an airtight container; it will last up to 3 days at room temperature or seven days in the fridge.

Nutrition Facts

Percent daily values based on the Reference Daily Intake (RDI) for a 2000 calorie diet.

Amount Per Serving

Calories 108.14 | Calories From Fat (2%) 2.27 | Total Fat 0.27g <1% | Saturated Fat 0.05g <1% | Cholesterol 0mg 0% | Sodium 89.22mg 4% | Potassium 99.35mg 3% | Total Carbohydrates 24.5g 8% | Fiber 1.5g 5% | Sugar 6.49g | Protein 2.69g 6%

Dark Cacao Banana Muffins

Ready in Time: 28 minutes | Servings: 12

Ingredients

non- stick baking spray

1/2 cup coconut butter softened

1 cup light brown sugar (packed)

4 Tbsp applesauce

2 bananas mashed

3 Tbsp coconut milk (canned)

2 cups of wheat flour all-purposed

1 tsp baking soda

Pinch of sea salt

1/3 cup cacao dry powder, unsweetened

1 cup toasted walnuts, chopped

1 cup water for Instant Pot

Instructions

1. Grease12 muffin cups (ceramic or silicon) with non-stick spray; set aside.
2. Add softened coconut butter and brown sugar in a mixing bowl.
3. Beat with an electric mixer until smooth and combined well.
4. Add the applesauce, banana, and coconut milk; continue to beat for the further 30 seconds.
5. Add in the flour, salt, and baking soda; beat on medium speed until all ingredients combined well.
6. Add the cacao powder and toasted walnuts; reduce speed to low, and continue to mix until combined well.
7. Pour the batter into prepared muffin cups.
8. Pour water to the inner stainless steel pot of your Instant Pot, and place the trivet inside.
9. Place muffin cups onto the trivet.
10. Lock lid into place and set on the MANUAL setting high pressure for 18 minutes.
11. Use the Quick Release valve to let the pressure out.
12. Remove muffins from the pot and allow to cool down completely.
13. Place muffins in a plastic bag, and store at room temperature for up to 3 days.
14. Or, place muffins into freezer bags and freeze for up to 3 months.
15. Before consuming, reheat your muffins in the microwave .
16. Microwave on HIGH about 30 seconds for each muffin.

Nutrition Facts

Percent daily values based on the Reference Daily Intake (RDI) for a 2000 calorie diet.

Amount Per Serving

Calories 320 | Calories From Fat (45%) 143.21 | Total Fat 16.84g 26% | Saturated Fat 9.41g 47% | Cholesterol 0mg 0% | Sodium 208.81mg 9% | Potassium 208.48mg 6% | Total Carbohydrates 41.77g 14% | Fiber 2.58g 10% | Sugar 21g | Protein 5.43g 10%

Darkwood Coconut Smoothie

Ready in Time: 10 minutes | Servings: 2

Ingredients

1 cup of fresh coconut meat finely chopped/sliced

1 1/2 cups of coconut milk

2 Tbsp of coconut butter

1 avocado (peeled, diced)

3 Tbsp cacao powder

2 tsp of cinnamon

1 scoop vegan protein powder (pea or soy protein)

1 Tbsp chia seeds

3 Tbsp strained or extracted honey

Instructions

1. Add all ingredients into a high-speed blender and blend until smooth.
2. Pour your smoothie into the bottle, glass, or Mason jars; cover and keep refrigerated up to 2 days.
3. Or, pour your smoothie into a freezer-safe Ziploc bag and freeze up to 3 months.
4. Let it defrost in the refrigerator overnight, stir and enjoy!

Nutrition Facts

Percent daily values based on the Reference Daily Intake (RDI) for a 2000 calorie diet.

Amount Per Serving

Calories 555.37 | Calories From Fat (38%) 389.16 | Total Fat 43.84g 74% | Saturated Fat 25.6g 70% | Cholesterol 0mg 0% | Sodium 50.22mg 2% | Potassium 1226.85mg 35% | Total Carbohydrates 61g 21% | Fiber 22.18g 89% | Sugar 27.7g | Protein 13.24g 26%

Delicious Seasoned Tomato Bread

Ready in Time: 45 minutes | Servings: 8

Ingredients

1 1/2 cups plain white flour
1 cup almond flour
1/2 tsp baking powder
1/2 tsp baking soda
1/2 tsp salt
1 1/2 tsp garlic powder
1 tsp dried onion powder
1 Tbsp dried basil
1/2 tsp dried oregano
4 Tbsp olive oil
3 Tbsp soy milk or almond milk
1 1/2 cups of pureed tomatoes (canned)
2 1/2 Tbsp tomato paste
1 Tbsp soy sauce

Instructions

1. Preheat your oven to 360 F.
2. Grease a loaf pan with olive oil; set aside.
3. Stir flours, baking powder and soda, salt, garlic, and onion powder, basil, and oregano in a large bowl.
4. In a separate bowl, stir all wet ingredients.
5. Fold the wet ingredients into the flour mixture, and stir until very well combined.
6. Pour the batter into a prepared baking loaf.
7. Bake for 35 minutes or until a toothpick inserted into the center comes out clean.
8. Remove from the oven and allow to cool down completely in the loaf pan.
9. Cover with a kitchen towel.
10. Cut the bread into slices, store into a container, and keep up to 3 days at room temperature.
11. Or, wrap bread slices, add into freezer bags, and freeze for longer-term storage.
12. Defrost a tomato bread slices; microwave them on high power for 20 to 25 seconds.

Nutrition Facts

Percent daily values based on the Reference Daily Intake (RDI) for a 2000 calorie diet.

Amount Per Serving

Calories 265.18 | Calories From Fat (52%) 137.72 | Total Fat 16.08g 25% | Saturated Fat 1.7g 8% | Cholesterol 0mg 0% | Sodium 428,05mg 18% | Potassium 314mg 9% | Total Carbohydrates 25.5g 9% | Fiber 3.54g 14% | Sugar 2.69g | Protein 7g 14%

Frozen Berries Vigor Smoothie

Ready in Time: 10 minutes | Servings: 2

Ingredients

1 1/2 cups almond milk

3/4 cup frozen berries, thawed (any)

1/2 cup fresh spinach leaves chopped

1 large banana sliced

3 Tbsp peanut butter

2 Tbsp strained honey

1 scoop vegan protein powder (soy)

Instructions

1. Add all ingredients in your blender, and blend until combined well.
2. Pour your smoothie into the bottle, glass, or Mason jars; cover and keep refrigerated up to 2 days.
3. Or, pour your smoothie into a freezer-safe Ziploc bag and freeze up to 3 months.
4. Let it defrost in the refrigerator overnight, stir and enjoy!

Nutrition Facts

Percent daily values based on the Reference Daily Intake (RDI) for a 2000 calorie diet.

Amount Per Serving

Calories 301 | Calories From Fat (38%) 113.68 | Total Fat 13.52g 21% | Saturated Fat 2.71g 14% | Cholesterol 1.16mg <1% | Sodium 137mg 6% | Potassium 570.22mg 16% | Total Carbohydrates 41.18g 14% | Fiber 4.72g 19% | Sugar 29.82g | Protein 10g 20%

Green Quinoa Breakfast Patties

Ready in Time: 20 minutes | Servings: 4

Ingredients

1 1/2 cup cooked quinoa

1/2 cup shredded carrots

1/2 cup shredded carrots

2 Tbsp flaxseed (soaked in 6 Tbsp water)

1/2 cup plain bread crumbs

2 garlic cloves minced

1 tsp onion powder

1 tsp garlic powder

2 Tbsp fresh parsley finely chopped

Salt and ground black pepper to taste

2 Tbsp extra virgin olive oil (plus additional for cooking)

Olive oil for frying

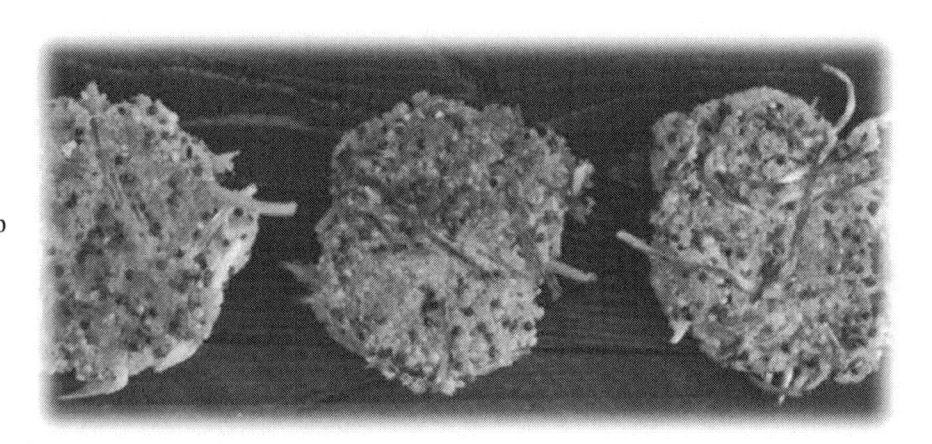

Instructions

1. In a large bowl, combine all ingredients until combined well.
2. Make patties out of the mixture.
3. Heat oil in a non-stick frying skillet.
4. Fry quinoa patties on both sides 2-3 minutes or until crisp.
5. Drain on a plate lined with a paper towel.
6. Keep refrigerated in an airtight container for up to 5 days.

Nutrition Facts

Percent daily values based on the Reference Daily Intake (RDI) for a 2000 calorie diet.

Amount Per Serving

Calories 155.38 | Calories From Fat (12%) 19.11 | Total Fat 2.15g 3% | Saturated Fat 0.18g <1% | Cholesterol 0mg 0% | Sodium 124.87mg 5% | Potassium 265.48mg 8% | Total Carbohydrates 28.8g 10% | Fiber 3.58g 14% | Sugar 2.23g | Protein 5.45g 11%

High Protein Chia and Banana Smoothie

Ready in Time: 10 minutes | Servings: 2

Ingredients

1 1/2 cup of coconut milk (canned)

2 Tbsp peanut butter, unsweetened

2 Tbsp chia seeds

1 cup celery leaves, finely chopped

1 large banana, sliced

1 scoop vegan protein powder (pea or soy protein)

2 Tbsp dark honey strained

Instructions

1. Add all ingredients into high-speed blender; blend until smooth and combined well.

2. Pour your smoothie into the bottle, glass, or Mason jars; cover and keep refrigerated up to 2 days.

3. Or, pour your smoothie into a freezer-safe Ziploc bag and freeze up to 3 months.

4. Let it defrost in the refrigerator overnight, stir and enjoy!

Nutrition Facts

Percent daily values based on the Reference Daily Intake (RDI) for a 2000 calorie diet.

Amount Per Serving

Calories 620,1 | Calories From Fat (66%) 406.92 | Total Fat 48.55g 75% | Saturated Fat 34.23g 171% | Cholesterol 1.16mg <1% | Sodium 129.3mg 5% | Potassium 861.45mg 25% | Total Carbohydrates 44.64g 15% | Fiber 7g 28% | Sugar 26.32g | Protein 12.68g 25%

Iced Salad and Pineapple Smoothie

Ready in Time: 10 minutes | Servings: 2

Ingredients

1 1/2 cups soy milk

2 Tbsp almond butter (plain, unsalted)

1 small head of lettuce chopped

1 cup raw pineapple chunks

1 large banana, cut into 1-inch pieces

1 scoop vegan protein powder (e.g., chia, soy or hemp)

2 Tbsp maple syrup

1 cup iced cubes (optional)

Instructions

1. Combine all ingredients in a blender and blend until smooth.
2. Pour your smoothie into the bottle, glass, or Mason jars; cover and keep refrigerated up to 2 days.
3. Or, pour your smoothie into a freezer-safe Ziploc bag and freeze up to 3 months.
4. Let it defrost in the refrigerator overnight, stir and enjoy!

Nutrition Facts

Percent daily values based on the Reference Daily Intake (RDI) for a 2000 calorie diet.

Amount Per Serving

Calories 368.7 | Calories From Fat (31%) 114.44 | Total Fat 13.36g 21% | Saturated Fat 1.2g 6% | Cholesterol 1.16mg <1% | Sodium 118.73mg 5% | Potassium 779.15mg 22% | Total Carbohydrates 54g 18% | Fiber 6.15g 25% | Sugar 36.27g | Protein 13.7g 28%

Dried Fruit Energy Bars

Ready in Time: 10 minutes | Servings: 4

Ingredients

1 cup dried plums chopped
1 cup pitted raisins
1 cup dried apricots chopped
3 Tbsp lemon juice
1 handful of chia seeds
2 Tbsp extracted honey

Instructions

1. Add all ingredients in your food processor; process it until getting a smooth mixture.
2. Apply the mixture in a baking sheet, and flat with a spatula; refrigerate the mixture for 2 hours.
3. Cut the mixture into bars.
4. Keep your energy bars tightly covered in the Ziploc bag in the refrigerator or freezer.

Nutrition Facts

Percent daily values based on the Reference Daily Intake (RDI) for a 2000 calorie diet.

Amount Per Serving

Calories 280.9 | Calories From Fat (2%) 4.23 | Total Fat 0.51g <1% | Saturated Fat 0.04g <1% | Cholesterol 0mg 0% | Sodium 12.61mg <1% | Potassium 900.12mg 26% | Total Carbohydrates 74.15g 25% | Fiber 5.9g 24% | Sugar 46.38g | Protein 3.1g 6%

Savory Storm White Smoothie

Ready in Time: 15 minutes | Servings: 2

Ingredients

2 cups steamed cauliflower florets
Pinch of salt
1 1/2 cups coconut milk (canned)
1 medium banana sliced
1 scoop vegan protein powder (pea, chia or soy protein)
2 Tbsp agave syrup or honey

Instructions

1. Rinse, clean and steam cauliflower florets with a pinch of salt for about 5 to 6 minutes; drain.
2. Add cauliflower into a high-speed blender along with all remaining ingredients.
3. Blend until smooth.
4. Pour your smoothie into the bottle, glass, or Mason jars; cover and keep refrigerated up to 2 days.
5. Or, pour your smoothie into a freezer-safe Ziploc bag and freeze up to 3 months.
6. Let it defrost in the refrigerator overnight, stir and enjoy!

Nutrition Facts

Percent daily values based on the Reference Daily Intake (RDI) for a 2000 calorie diet.

Amount Per Serving

Calories 486 | Calories From Fat (65%) 315.23 | Total Fat 37.58g 58% | Saturated Fat 32.28g 161% | Cholesterol 1.16mg <1% | Sodium 73.12mg 3% | Potassium 987.62mg 28% | Total Carbohydrates 37.63g 13% | Fiber 4g 16% | Sugar 21.53g | Protein 8.71g 18%

Simple Vegan Waffles

Ready in Time: 20 minutes | Servings: 4

Ingredients

1 1/2 cups whole wheat flour (of any GF flour)

2 Tbs natural brown sugar

1 tsp baking soda

1 tsp baking powder

pinch of salt

1 tsp of protein powder

1 1/2 cups of almond milk

4 Tbsp virgin olive oil

Instructions

1. First, preheat your waffle maker according to manufacturers instructions.
2. Combine all ingredients in a bowl and stir until combine well.
3. Pour the half of the cup of batter in the center of the waffle maker.
4. Close the cover and wait until the light turns green.
5. Remove waffles on the warm plate and cover with kitchen paper.
6. Repeat this process with the rest of the batter.
7. Store waffles in an airtight container in refrigerate up to 3 days.
8. Or freeze your waffles in a freezer-safe bag/s up to two months.
9. Reheat your waffles in the oven at 350 F for 10 to 15 minutes.

Nutrition Facts

Percent daily values based on the Reference Daily Intake (RDI) for a 2000 calorie diet.

Amount Per Serving

Calories 230.38 | Calories From Fat (11%) 25.51 | Total Fat 2.49g 4% | Saturated Fat 0.09g <1% | Cholesterol 0.19mg <1% | Sodium 547.43mg 23% | Potassium 69.8mg 2% | Total Carbohydrates 44.13g 15% | Fiber 1.33g 5% | Sugar 6.85g | Protein 6g 12%

Spicy Vegan Breakfast Smoothie

Ready in Time: 10 minutes | Servings: 2

Ingredients

1 large banana sliced
1/2 cup of kale
1 cup of apple juice
1/2 cup of frozen berries (any)
2 to 3 Tbs almond butter
1/2 tsp grated ginger
1/2 tsp turmeric
1/4 tsp of cinnamon
1/4 tsp of cumin
1 scoop vegan protein powder (e.g., chia, soy or hemp)

Instructions

1. Add all ingredients in your blender; blend until smooth well.
2. Pour your smoothie into the bottle, glass, or Mason jars; cover and keep refrigerated up to 2 days.
3. Or, pour your smoothie into a freezer-safe Ziploc bag and freeze up to 3 months.
4. Let it defrost in the refrigerator overnight, stir and enjoy!

Nutrition Facts

Percent daily values based on the Reference Daily Intake (RDI) for a 2000 calorie diet.

Amount Per Serving

Calories 276.3 | Calories From Fat (42%) 115.16 | Total Fat 13.11g 20% | Saturated Fat 7.5g 38% | Cholesterol 31.69mg 11% | Sodium 29.82mg 1% | Potassium 583.68mg 17% | Total Carbohydrates 37.47g 13% | Fiber 4.34g 17% | Sugar 27.43g | Protein 4.72g 10%

Total Almond & Ginger Pear Cake

Ready in Time: 45 minutes | Servings: 12

Ingredients

1 Tbsp avocado or olive oil

2 cups all-purpose flour

1 cup granulated sugar

1 1/2 tsp baking powder

1 Tbsp ground ginger

Pinch of salt

1/2 cup almond butter (plain, unsalted)

2 large pears cut into small dices

1/2 cup almonds, toasted and roughly chopped

2/3 cup almond milk

1 Tbsp applesauce canned

Instructions

1. Heat oven to 360 F.
2. Grease a baking dish with oil and set aside.
3. In a large bowl, stir flour and all dry ingredients.
4. Add almond butter and pears, and stir well.
5. Add all remaining ingredients and beat with a mixer on low until well combined.
6. Pour mixture into prepared baking dish.
7. Bake cake for 30 to 35 minutes or until a skewer inserted into the middle comes out almost clean.
8. Remove cake to a wire rack to completely cool.
9. Cut cake and store in an airtight container; keep
10. Keep it in a cool place for two days or refrigerate up to 5 days.

Nutrition Facts

Percent daily values based on the Reference Daily Intake (RDI) for a 2000 calorie diet.

Amount Per Serving

Calories 294 | Calories From Fat (29%) 85.7 | Total Fat 10.2g 16% | Saturated Fat 0.86g 4% | Cholesterol 0mg 0% | Sodium 160.12mg 7% | Potassium 230.36mg 7% | Total Carbohydrates 47.6g 16% | Fiber 4.56g 18% | Sugar 24.8g | Protein 5.83g 12%

Vegan Spinach Artichoke Quiche with Tofu

Ready in Time: 1 hour and 5 minutes | Servings: 6

Ingredients

2 large tortillas (gluten-free if needed)
non-stick cooking olive oil spray
2 Tbsp olive oil
1 small onion chopped
2 cloves of garlic minced
Salt and ground black pepper to taste
2 cups of fresh spinach
1 cup of soft tofu
4 Tbsp nutritional yeast
1 Tbsp yellow mustard
1 lemon juiced
1 tsp fresh parsley finely chopped
1 tsp fresh basil finely chopped
1 can (14 oz) artichoke hearts drained and chopped

Instructions

1. Preheat oven to 350 F.
2. Grease a baking pie dish with non-stick olive oil spray.
3. Chop tortillas and cover the baking dish evenly; sprinkle with some oil and set aside.
4. Heat olive oil in a frying skillet over medium-high heat.
5. Saute the onion and garlic with the pinch salt and pepper until soft or for about 3 to 4 minutes.
6. Add spinach and cook, occasionally stirring, for further 3 minutes or until spinach is wilted.
7. Remove from the heat and set aside.
8. Add tofu, nutritional yeast, mustard, lemon juice, parsley, and basil into a food processor; process until smooth and well combined.
9. Add artichoke hearts, and the onion mixture and process until combined well.
10. Pour artichoke mixture into a prepared baking dish with tortillas.
11. Bake for 40 to 45 minutes.
12. Remove from the oven and allow it to cool down completely.
13. Wrap a baking dish into aluminum foil and keep refrigerated up to 3 or 4 days.
14. If you slice your quiche, place individual slices into resealable plastic bags.
15. If you want to freeze your quiche, place the whole quiche into a freezer bag, and keep up to 1 month.
16. When you want to eat your quiche, reheat it in a pre-heated oven on 350 F for about 30 minutes.

Nutrition Facts

Percent daily values based on the Reference Daily Intake (RDI) for a 2000 calorie diet.

Amount Per Serving

Calories 130.2 | Calories From Fat (43%) 55.79 | Total Fat 6.41g 10% | Saturated Fat 0.83g 4% | Cholesterol 0mg 0% | Sodium 107mg 4% | Potassium 441.24mg 13% | Total Carbohydrates 14.54g 5% | Fiber 6.58g 26% | Sugar 1.27g | Protein 7.82g 16%

LUNCH

Aromatic Spinach with Basil-Sesame Puree

Ready in Time: 30 minutes | Servings: 4

Ingredients

1 lb fresh spinach
4 Tbsp of olive oil
1 onion finely chopped
1 leek finely chopped
3 cloves garlic
3 cup of vegetable broth
4 Tbsp grated tomato
1 cup fresh basil finely chopped
1/3 cup sesame oil
Salt and ground pepper to taste

Instructions

1. Boil spinach in salted water for 3 to 5 minutes.
2. Remove from heat and place in colander to drain.
3. Heat oil in a frying skillet over medium-high heat.
4. Sauté the onion, leek, and garlic with a pinch of salt, often stirring, for about 5 to 6 minutes.
5. Pour vegetable broth, grated tomato, and basil leaves; stir for 2 minutes.
6. Add spinach, give a good stir, cover, and cook for 6 - 8 minutes over medium-low heat.
7. Transfer the spinach mixture in a blender, and add the sesame oil; blend for 30 seconds or until smooth.
8. Taste and adjust salt and pepper.
9. Store in an airtight container and freeze for a month.

Nutrition Facts

Percent daily values based on the Reference Daily Intake (RDI) for a 2000 calorie diet.

Amount Per Serving

Calories 381.85 | Calories From Fat (77%) 295.2 | Total Fat 33.53g 52% | Saturated Fat 4.68g 23% | Cholesterol 0.46mg <1% | Sodium 843.36mg 35% | Potassium 552.58mg 16% | Total Carbohydrates 17.7g 6% | Fiber 6g 24% | Sugar 3.14g | Protein 6.76g 14%

Baked Quinoa and Black Beans Patties

Ready in Time: 1 hour and 5 minutes | Servings: 2

Ingredients

1 cup of quinoa

1 cup of water

1 can (15 oz) of black beans

4 Tbsp sesame seeds

4 Tbsp bread crumbs

2 Tbsp tomato paste

1 Tbsp hot sauce (any)

2 Tbsp nutritional yeast

1 tsp garlic powder

1/2 tsp of oregano

1/2 tsp of rosemary

1 Tbsp fresh basil finely chopped

Salt and ground black pepper to taste

Instructions

1. In a pot, cook quinoa for about 15 minutes.
2. Place in a colander, and drain; let quinoa to cool down.
3. Preheat oven to 400 F.
4. Line a baking sheet with baking paper.
5. In a bowl, add black beans and mash with a fork.
6. Add quinoa, sesame seeds, and all remaining ingredients; stir until combine well.
7. Roll dough into balls.
8. Place quinoa balls/patties on a prepared baking sheet.
9. Bake for about 35 minutes.
10. Remove from the oven, and allow to cool completely.
11. Store in an airtight container and keep refrigerated up to 4 to 5 days.

Yield: 4 large patties

Nutrition Facts

Percent daily values based on the Reference Daily Intake (RDI) for a 2000 calorie diet.

Amount Per Serving

Calories 614,39 | Calories From Fat (21%) 130,31 | Total Fat 15.29g 24% | Saturated Fat 2.51g 13% | Cholesterol 0.21mg <1% | Sodium 719.14mg 30% | Potassium 1312.62mg 39% | Total Carbohydrates 93.57g 31% | Fiber 25g 100% | Sugar 5.48g | Protein 32g 64%

Barley and Broccoli Pilaf

Ready in Time: 55 minutes | Servings: 4

Ingredients

4 Tbsp olive oil

1 onion, chopped

salt and fresh ground pepper to taste

1 cup pearled barley

2 cups of vegan vegetable broth

1 cup of water

1 tsp fresh thyme

1 1/2 cup broccoli florets, cut into small pieces

1/4 cup green peas

1 carrot finely sliced

1 tomato sliced

Instructions

1. Heat oil in a large frying pan; sauté onion with a pinch of salt for 2 to 3 minutes.
2. Add barley and constantly stir for a further 2 minutes.
3. Add vegetable broth, thyme, and water and bring to boil.
4. Cover, reduce heat to low and simmer for 30 minutes.
5. Add all remaining ingredients, stir well, and cook for further 20 minutes.
6. Taste and adjust the salt and pepper to taste.
7. Allow it to cool completely.
8. Store barley pilaf in an airtight container and keep refrigerated up to 5 days.
9. Or, place in freezer bags and keep in the freezer for one month.

Nutrition Facts

Percent daily values based on the Reference Daily Intake (RDI) for a 2000 calorie diet.

Amount Per Serving

Calories 409.46 | Calories From Fat (37%) 151.2 | Total Fat 17.15g 26% | Saturated Fat 2.51g 13% | Cholesterol 0.62mg <1% | Sodium 635.47mg 26% | Potassium 588.46mg 17% | Total Carbohydrates 58.38g 19% | Fiber 11.61g 46% | Sugar 5.36g | Protein 8.63g 17%

Cabbage and Cauliflower Puree

Ready in Time: 30 minutes | Servings: 4

Ingredients

water for cooking

1/2 medium head cabbage

1/2 lb cauliflower florets

1 leek finely sliced

2 stalks fresh celery chopped

4 Tbsp olive oil

Salt and pepper to taste

Instructions

1. Heat water (about 4 1/2 cups) in a big pot and add all vegetables and oil; season with the little salt.

2. Bring to boil, reduce heat to medium, cover, and cook for about 15 -20 minutes.

3. Transfer vegetables in a blender; blend until smooth and combined well.

4. Taste and adjust the salt and pepper to taste.

5. Store in an airtight container and keep refrigerated up to 3 to 4 days.

Nutrition Facts

Percent daily values based on the Reference Daily Intake (RDI) for a 2000 calorie diet.

Amount Per Serving

Calories 176.15 | Calories From Fat (69%) 122.33 | Total Fat 13.85g 21% | Saturated Fat 2g 10% | Cholesterol 0mg 0% | Sodium 43.22mg 2% | Potassium 413.19mg 12% | Total Carbohydrates 12.7g 4% | Fiber 4.43g 18% | Sugar 5.6g | Protein 3g 6%

Dark Red Vegan Soup

Ready in Time: 1 hour and 10 minutes | Servings: 4

Ingredients

4 Tbsp olive oil

1 onion finely diced

2 cloves garlic finely chopped

salt and freshly ground black pepper

1 lb tomatoes, peeled and grated

2 beets, large, peeled and cut into pieces

2 carrots cut into strips

3/4 tsp cumin

1 tsp cayenne pepper

4 cups of vegetable broth

Instructions

1. Heat the oil in a large pot on medium-high temperature.

2. Add the onion and garlic and sauté with the pinch of salt, often stirring, for about 3 to 4 minutes.

3. Add grated tomatoes, beets, and carrots, and stir for 2 to 3 minutes.

4. Add all remaining ingredients and stir well.

5. Reduce heat to medium-low, cover, and cook for about 50 to 60 minutes.

6. Remove from heat; taste and adjust the salt and pepper to taste.

7. Allow to cool down and store in an airtight container; keep refrigerated up to 5 days.

Nutrition Facts

Percent daily values based on the Reference Daily Intake (RDI) for a 2000 calorie diet.

Amount Per Serving

Calories 162.24 | Calories From Fat (15%) 23.79 | Total Fat 2.69g 4% | Saturated Fat 0.58g 3% | Cholesterol 1.38mg <1% | Sodium 982.38mg 41% | Potassium 808.6mg 23% | Total Carbohydrates 30.6g 10% | Fiber 6g 24% | Sugar 9g | Protein 6g 12%

Delicious Breaded Tofu Sticks

Ready in Time: 25 minutes | Servings: 4

Ingredients

1 block extra-firm tofu, well-drained (16 ounces)

4 cloves garlic finely minced

1 Tbsp of mustard

1 Tbsp corn syrup

2 Tbsp tomato paste

1 Tbsp tamari sauce

1 Tbsp water

Salt and ground black pepper to taste

3/4 cup breadcrumbs

1/2 cup of sesame oil for frying

Instructions

1. Drain well the tofu, and cut into strips/pieces/sticks; set aside.
2. Whisk the minced garlic, mustard, corn syrup, tomato paste, tamari sauce, water, and the salt and the pepper in one bowl.
3. In a separate dish/bowl, add the breadcrumbs.
4. Dip the tofu steaks evenly in the garlic mixture.
5. Then, dip your tofu steak into the breadcrumbs.
6. Heat the oil in a frying skillet over medium heat.
7. Fry breaded tofu for about 5 minutes per side; gently flips tofu once.
8. Remove tofu on a plate lined with a paper towel, and allow to drain and cool completely.
9. Store in an airtight container and keep refrigerated up to 3 to 4 days.

Nutrition Facts

Percent daily values based on the Reference Daily Intake (RDI) for a 2000 calorie diet.

Amount Per Serving

Calories 456.33 | Calories From Fat (67%) 307.42 | Total Fat 35.17g 54% | Saturated Fat 4.75g 24% | Cholesterol 0mg 0% | Sodium 524.33mg 22% | Potassium 298.4mg 9% | Total Carbohydrates 24.1g 8% | Fiber 2g 8% | Sugar 4.4g | Protein 15.11g 30%

Eggplant and Parsley Puree

Ready in Time: 20 minutes | Servings: 6

Ingredients

2 lbs eggplants cut into cubes

1 cup fresh parsley leaves

3 cloves garlic, minced

1 green bell pepper, cored and roughly chopped

2 cup of water

1 cup of extra-virgin olive oil

2 Tbsp fresh lemon juice (2 lemons)

Salt and freshly ground black pepper, to taste

Instructions

1. Peel and rinse eggplant; cut eggplant in cubes, and add into Instant pot along with garlic, green pepper, and parsley, and water.

2. Lock lid into place and set on the MANUAL setting high pressure for 5 minutes.

3. When the beep sounds, quick release the pressure by pressing Cancel, and twisting the steam handle to the Venting position.

4. Transfer vegetables into a blender along with oil, lemon juice, and the salt and pepper to taste.

5. Blend until smooth and well combined.

6. Store in an airtight container and keep refrigerated up to 3 to 4 days.

Nutrition Facts

Percent daily values based on the Reference Daily Intake (RDI) for a 2000 calorie diet.

Amount Per Serving

Calories 167.31 | Calories From Fat (95%) 159.3 | Total Fat 18g 28% | Saturated Fat 2.5g 13% | Cholesterol 0mg 0% | Sodium 1.39mg <1% | Potassium 53.6mg 2% | Total Carbohydrates 2g <1% | Fiber 0.46g 2% | Sugar 0.72g | Protein 0.32g <1%

Fresh Garden Vegetable Soup

Ready in Time: 20 minutes | Servings: 5

Ingredients

4 Tbsp olive oil
1 onion finely diced
2 cloves garlic finely sliced
Salt and ground black pepper to taste
2 carrots, peeled and sliced
2 celery sticks, sliced
1 cup kale leaves chopped
1 zucchini, diced
1 cup dried mushrooms
1 cup tomatoes peeled and grated
4 cups vegetable broth
1 bay leaf
1 tsp fresh parsley leaves
1 tsp fresh basil leaves

Instructions

1. Turn on the Instant Pot and press the SAUTÉ button.
2. Add olive oil, and sauté onion, and garlic with the pinch of salt for about 2 to 3 minutes.
3. Add sliced carrots and celery, and stir for one minute.
4. Add kale, zucchini, and mushrooms; stir for one minute.
5. Add grated tomatoes, and stir well.
6. Add the vegetable broth along with all remaining ingredients, and stir well.
7. Lock lid into place and set on the MANUAL setting high pressure for 5 minutes.
8. Once the pot beeps finished, use a Quick release.
9. Taste and adjust the salt and pepper to taste.
10. Allow soup to cool completely.
11. Store soup in an airtight container, and refrigerate up to 5 days or freeze up to two months.

Nutrition Facts

Percent daily values based on the Reference Daily Intake (RDI) for a 2000 calorie diet.

Amount Per Serving

Calories 262.92 | Calories From Fat (48%) 126.6 | Total Fat 14.31g 22% | Saturated Fat 2.28g 11% | Cholesterol 1.97mg <1% | Sodium 1329.49mg 55% | Potassium 681.1mg 19% | Total Carbohydrates 28.68g 10% | Fiber 4.64g 19% | Sugar 2.79g | Protein 7g 14%

Fried Tofu with Asparagus and Chinese Sauce

Ready in Time: 25 minutes | Servings: 4

Ingredients

14 oz extra firm tofu

3 Tbsp sesame oil

1 Tbsp soy sauce

1 lb of asparagus cut into 2-inch long pieces

2 Tbsp green onions finely chopped

For the Sauce:

4 Tbsp Tamari sauce (or soy sauce)

4 Tbsp sesame oil

2 Tbsp rice vinegar

4 cloves garlic minced

1 tsp ginger freshly grated

1/4 cup brown sugar

Instructions

1. Cut the block of tofu in half.
2. Gently press tofu halves between paper towels to remove any liquid; cut the tofu into 1/2-inch cubes.
3. Heat oil in a large wok/frying skillet over medium-high heat.
4. Fry tofu cubes until tofu are lightly golden brown
5. Add soy sauce and toss to combine well.
6. Transfer tofu in a bowl, and set aside.
7. In the same wok/frying skillet sauté asparagus and green onions until soft.
8. Transfer vegetables in a bowl with tofu.
9. Whisk all sauce ingredients in a bowl until combined well.
10. Pour sauce over vegetables and tofu, and toss to combine well.
11. Taste and adjust seasonings if needed.
12. Store in an airtight container and keep refrigerated up to 4 to 5 days.

Nutrition Facts

Percent daily values based on the Reference Daily Intake (RDI) for a 2000 calorie diet.

Amount Per Serving

Calories 386.14 | Calories From Fat (67%) 259.3 | Total Fat 29.71g 46% | Saturated Fat 4g 20% | Cholesterol 0mg 0% | Sodium 1153.52mg 48% | Potassium 405.92mg 12% | Total Carbohydrates 23.88g 8% | Fiber 2.13g 9% | Sugar 15.58g | Protein 13.6g 27%

Fried Tomato Sauce

Ready in Time: 40 minutes | Servings: 8

Ingredients

4 Tbsp virgin olive oil
1 small onion finely diced
2 cloves chopped garlic
3 lbs of tomatoes, peeled, seeded, and chopped
salt and ground pepper to taste
1/2 cup of ground almonds
1 bay leaf
2 sprigs of parsley
1/2 cup vegetable broth

Instructions

1. Heat oil in a large pot and sauté the onion and garlic with a pinch of salt and pepper until soft.
2. Add tomatoes and cook, often stirring on high heat for 2 to 3 minutes.
3. Add all remaining ingredients and bring to boil.
4. Reduce heat to medium-low, cover, and cook for 15 - 20 minutes.
5. Transfer mixture to a blender; blend the mixture with an immersion blender until soft.
6. Allow the sauce to cool completely, store in a container, and keep refrigerated up to a week.
7. Also, you can freeze your sauce in a freezer bag for up to 3 months

Nutrition Facts

Percent daily values based on the Reference Daily Intake (RDI) for a 2000 calorie diet.

Amount Per Serving

Calories 161 | Calories From Fat (62%) 100.33 | Total Fat 11.6g 18% | Saturated Fat 1.34g 7% | Cholesterol 0mg 0% | Sodium 46.86mg 2% | Potassium 501.7mg 14% | Total Carbohydrates 10.53g 4% | Fiber 3.27g 13% | Sugar 5.7g | Protein 3.55g 7%

Hearty and Creamy Corn Chowder

Ready in Time: 20 minutes | Servings: 4

Ingredients

2 cups of frozen whole kernel corn
2 Tbsp chopped onion
1 tsp of grated garlic
2 Tbsp finely chopped parsley
4 Tbsp chopped green pepper
1 1/2 cups of vegetable broth
2 Tbsp olive oil
Salt and ground pepper to taste
1 cup of almond milk
2 Tbsp yellow cornmeal

Instructions

1. Add corn, onion, garlic, parsley, green pepper, salt and pepper, vegetable broth, and olive oil in your Instant Pot; stir.
2. Dissolve cornmeal in almond milk and pour in Instant pot; give a good stir.
3. Lock lid into place and set on the MANUAL setting high pressure for 10 minutes.
4. When the timer beeps, press "Cancel" and carefully flip the Quick Release valve to let the pressure out.
5. Taste and adjust the salt and pepper to taste; allow to cool completely.
6. Store your chowder in an airtight container, and keep refrigerated up to 4 days.

Note: *For quick and easy reheating, store single-serving portions in individual containers.*

Nutrition Facts

Percent daily values based on the Reference Daily Intake (RDI) for a 2000 calorie diet.

Amount Per Serving

Calories 225.14 | Calories From Fat (39%) 86.92 | Total Fat 9.67g 15% | Saturated Fat 1.2g 6% | Cholesterol 0mg 0% | Sodium 448mg 19% | Potassium 456.18mg 13% | Total Carbohydrates 32.58g 11% | Fiber 4g 16% | Sugar 4.6g | Protein 6.7g 14%

High-protein Quinoa with Celery and Pine Nuts

Ready in Time: 25 minutes | Servings: 4

Ingredients

4 Tbsp olive oil
2 green onions sliced
1 cup quinoa
1/4 cup pine nuts
4 stalks celery, chopped
3 cups vegetable broth
Sea salt to taste
1/4 cup fresh lemon juice
1/4 tsp cayenne pepper
1/2 tsp ground cumin
2 Tbsp fresh parsley chopped

Instructions

1. Turn on the Instant Pot and press the SAUTÉ button and heat oil.
2. Sauté the green onion with a pinch of salt until soft.
3. Add quinoa and peanuts, and stir for one minute.
4. Add celery, and all remaining ingredients and give a good stir.
5. Lock lid into place and set on the MANUAL setting high pressure for 3 minutes.
6. Once the pot beeps finished, use a natural release for 10 minutes.
7. Remove from the pot and allow to cool down.
8. Store in an airtight container in a fridge for up to 5 days.

Nutrition Facts

Percent daily values based on the Reference Daily Intake (RDI) for a 2000 calorie diet.

Amount Per Serving

Calories 470.37 | Calories From Fat (46%) 218.64 | Total Fat 24.6g 38% | Saturated Fat 3.28g 16% | Cholesterol 1.85mg <1% | Sodium 1602.8mg 67% | Potassium 751.2mg 21% | Total Carbohydrates 51.52g 17% | Fiber 6.79g 27% | Sugar 1.73g | Protein 12.56g 25%

Instant Fava Bean Soup with Saffron

Ready in Time: 40 minutes | Servings: 4

Ingredients

4 Tbsp olive oil

1 yellow onion finely diced

2 cloves garlic, chopped

Kosher salt and freshly ground black pepper, to taste

1 1/2 cups Fava Bean (broad beans)

1 can (11 oz) tomatoes - diced

4 cups vegetable broth

1 tsp crushed saffron threads (or 1/2 tsp of ground turmeric)

1 tsp ground cumin

Instructions

1. Turn on the Instant Pot and press the SAUTÉ button; heat oil.
2. Sauté onion and garlic with the pinch of salt, often stirring, for about 2 to 3 minutes.
3. Add fava beans and tomatoes; stir for one minute.
4. Add the vegetable broth, and all remaining ingredients, and stir well.
5. Lock lid into place and set on the MANUAL setting high pressure for 30 minutes.
6. Use Quick Release - turn the valve from sealing to venting to release the pressure.
7. Allow it to cool completely.
8. Store in an airtight container and keep refrigerated up to 4 to 5 days.
9. You can also freeze your fava beans soup in freezer bags for up to six months.

Nutrition Facts

Percent daily values based on the Reference Daily Intake (RDI) for a 2000 calorie diet.

Amount Per Serving

Calories 331.33 | Calories From Fat (46%) 153.58 | Total Fat 17.37g 27% | Saturated Fat 2.72g 14% | Cholesterol 2.15mg <1% | Sodium 1548.13mg 65% | Potassium 695.25mg 20% | Total Carbohydrates 37.2g 13% | Fiber 4.14g 17% | Sugar 3.17g | Protein 10g 20%

Instant Lentils Bolognese

Ready in Time: 35 minutes | Servings: 5

Ingredients

4 Tbsp olive oil

1 large onion

2 cloves garlic finely chopped

Salt and ground pepper to taste

2 cup of red lentils

1 carrot sliced

1 can (15 oz) peeled tomatoes

4 cups of vegetable broth

1 Tbsp Italian seasoning

Instructions

1. Press the SAUTÉ button on your Instant Pot, and add oil.

2. Sauté the onion and garlic with a pinch of salt until soft or for about 3 minutes.

3. Add lentils and stir for a further one minute.

4. Add carrots and tomatoes, and stir for one minute.

5. Add broth and Italian seasoning.

6. Lock lid into place and set on the MANUAL setting high pressure for 15 minutes.

7. Once cooking completes, let the pressure valve release naturally (about 10 minutes), and quick-release remaining pressure.

8. Taste and adjust seasonings; allow it to cool completely.

9. Store in a covered glass or airtight container in the fridge for up to 4 days.

10. Or, you can freeze your lentils for two months.

Nutrition Facts

Percent daily values based on the Reference Daily Intake (RDI) for a 2000 calorie diet.

Amount Per Serving

Calories 522.2 | Calories From Fat (25%) 131.53 | Total Fat 14.85g 23% | Saturated Fat 2.34g 12% | Cholesterol 2mg <1% | Sodium 1372.65mg 57% | Potassium 1206.23mg 34% | Total Carbohydrates 73.36g 24% | Fiber 27.37g 109% | Sugar 4.28g | Protein 25.42g 51%

Jasmine Rice and Peas Risotto

Ready in Time: 25 minutes | Servings: 4

Ingredients

4 Tbsp olive oil
1 medium onion finely diced
2 cloves garlic minced
Salt and ground black pepper to taste
1 1/2 cups dry jasmine rice (or long grain rice)
1/2 cup of green peas
1 bay leaf
2 cups of vegetable broth
2 cups of water

Instructions

1. Press the SAUTÉ button on your Instant Pot.
2. When the word "hot" appears on display, add the oil and sauté the onion and garlic with a pinch of salt for about 5 minutes; stir frequently.
3. Add the jasmine rice and stir for one minute.
4. Add green peas, and all remaining ingredients and stir well.
5. Lock lid into place and set on the RICE setting high pressure for 6 minutes.
6. When the timer beeps, press "Cancel" and use a Natural release for 10 to 15 minutes.
7. Taste and adjust the salt and pepper to taste.
8. Allow cooling completely.
9. Store your risotto in an airtight container, and keep refrigerated up to 4 to 5 days.

Nutrition Facts

Percent daily values based on the Reference Daily Intake (RDI) for a 2000 calorie diet.

Amount Per Serving

Calories 421 | Calories From Fat (34%) 144.5 | Total Fat 16.58g 26% | Saturated Fat 2.1g 11% | Cholesterol 0mg 0% | Sodium 59.4mg 2% | Potassium 181mg 5% | Total Carbohydrates 67.1g 22% | Fiber 5.81g 23% | Sugar 2.3g | Protein 8.21g 16%

Simple Lentil Soup

Ready in Time: 35 minutes | Servings: 6

Ingredients

4 Tbsp olive oil

1 medium onion, chopped

2 cloves garlic minced

3/4 tsp kosher salt and fresh ground black pepper

1 1/2 cups mature seeds lentils

2 large carrots sliced

1 medium potato, peeled and diced

1 cup tomato juice

4 cups vegetable broth

2 bay leaves

2 Tbsp fresh thyme finely chopped

Instructions

1. Turn on the Instant Pot and press the SAUTÉ button.
2. When the word "hot" appears on display, add the oil and sauté the onions and garlic with a pinch of salt and pepper for about 2 to 3 minutes.
3. Add lentils, carrot, and potato and stir for one minute.
4. Pour the tomato juice, broth, and all remaining ingredients; stir for one minute.
5. Lock lid into place and set on the MANUAL setting high pressure for 15 minutes.
6. Release pressure naturally for 10 minutes and quick-release remaining pressure.
7. Taste and adjust seasonings to taste; allow soup to cool completely.
8. Store soup in an airtight container and refrigerate for up to 3 days.
9. Or, pour soup into freezer bags, and freeze for one month.

Nutrition Facts

Percent daily values based on the Reference Daily Intake (RDI) for a 2000 calorie diet.

Amount Per Serving

Calories 409.1 | Calories From Fat (26%) 108.2 | Total Fat 12.21g 19% | Saturated Fat 2g 10% | Cholesterol 1.64mg <1% | Sodium 1347.3mg 56% | Potassium 1061.31mg 30% | Total Carbohydrates 58.44g 19% | Fiber 18.81g 75% | Sugar 4.81g | Protein 17.85g 36%

Oven-baked Peas Fritters

Ready in Time: 35 minutes | Servings: 4

Ingredients

4 Tbsp olive oil
1 onion, finely diced
2 garlic cloves, minced
A pinch of salt and ground black pepper
2 cups boiled peas, drained
1 1/2 cups chickpea flour
1 tsp baking soda
1/2 tsp turmeric
2 Tbsp Italian seasonings

Instructions

1. Preheat your oven 350F.
2. Line a baking tray with baking paper; set aside.
3. Heat oil in a frying skillet, and sauté the onion with a pinch of salt until softened.
4. Add drained peas, and stir for a further two minutes.
5. Add the mixture to a food processor and pulse until combined well.
6. Stir in the chickpea flour, soda, turmeric, salt, pepper, and Italian seasoning.
7. Shape the mixture into round balls/patties; arrange balls/patties onto a prepared baking tray.
8. Bake for 16 to18 minutes or until golden brown.
9. Remove from the oven, and allow fritters to cool completely.
10. Store your fritters in an airtight container and keep refrigerated for up to 3 days or freeze them up to a month.
11. To reheat frozen fritters, place them on a baking paper-lined sheet and heat on a 400 F oven for 15 minutes.

Nutrition Facts

Percent daily values based on the Reference Daily Intake (RDI) for a 2000 calorie diet.

Amount Per Serving

Calories 415.14 | Calories From Fat (36%) 151 | Total Fat 17.28g 27% | Saturated Fat 2.28g 11% | Cholesterol 0mg 0% | Sodium 703.8mg 29% | Potassium 557.92mg 16% | Total Carbohydrates 51.44g 17% | Fiber 9.66g 39% | Sugar 5.45g | Protein 14.2g 28%

Robust Potato, Rice, and Spinach Soup

Ready in Time: 25 minutes | Servings: 6

Ingredients

4 Tbsp olive oil

4 sliced leeks

3 crushed garlic cloves

1 tsp salt and ground black pepper to taste

1 cup rice long grained

3 potatoes (cut in large chunks)

4 cups vegetable broth

1 cup fresh spinach

1/4 cup fresh parsley finely chopped

1/4 cup fresh celery finely chopped

2 Tbsp fresh lemon juice

2 Tbsp tomato paste

1 bay leaf

2 tsp dried basil

Instructions

1. Turn on the Instant Pot and press the SAUTÉ button; heat oil.
2. Sauté leeks and garlic with the pinch of salt, occasionally stirring, for about 3 to 4 minutes.
3. Add rice and potato, and stir for about 2 minutes.
4. Add spinach and all remaining ingredients and stir well.
5. Lock lid into place and set on the MANUAL setting high pressure for 8 minutes.
6. Allow the pressure to release naturally for 10 minutes and then release any remaining pressure.
7. Once all of the pressure releases, the steam will no longer come out of the vent, and you'll be able to open the lid.
8. Taste and adjust the salt and pepper.
9. Refrigerate cooked soup in an airtight container up to 5 days.
10. Or, freeze in heavy-duty freezer bags for up to one month.

Nutrition Facts

Percent daily values based on the Reference Daily Intake (RDI) for a 2000 calorie diet.

Amount Per Serving

Calories 365.17 | Calories From Fat (29%) 106.3 | Total Fat 12g 18% | Saturated Fat 1.93g 10% | Cholesterol 1.64mg <1% | Sodium 1542.4mg 64% | Potassium 899mg 26% | Total Carbohydrates 57.51g 19% | Fiber 5.94g 24% | Sugar 3.8g | Protein 8.5g 17%

Spiced Cabbage, Soybeans and Peanuts Stew

Ready in Time: 15 minutes | Servings: 4

Instructions

3 cups cabbage, finely chopped

3/4 cup of soybeans in the pod

2 large carrots sliced

1 small red pepper, diced

1 Tbsp minced garlic

1/2 cup of peanuts

1/4 cup of olive oil

salt and pepper, to taste

1/4 cup of soy sauce

1/2 cup of water

1 lime freshly juiced

1/4 tsp of garlic powder

1/4 tsp of ginger powder

Instructions

1. Add all ingredients in an 8-quart Instant Pot.
2. Stir to combine well.
3. Lock lid into place and set on the MANUAL setting for 8 minutes.
4. When the beep sounds, quick release the pressure by pressing Cancel, and twisting the steam handle to the Venting position.
5. Once all of the pressure releases, the steam will no longer come out of the vent, and you'll be able to open the lid.
6. Taste and adjust seasonings; leave it to cool completely.
7. Keep refrigerated in an airtight container up to 3 days or freeze in freezer bags up to 2 months.

Nutrition Facts

Percent daily values based on the Reference Daily Intake (RDI) for a 2000 calorie diet.

Amount Per Serving

Calories 351 | Calories From Fat (58%) 203.43 | Total Fat 23.4g 36% | Saturated Fat 3.24g 16% | Cholesterol 0mg 0% | Sodium 744.31mg 31% | Potassium 535.31mg 15% | Total Carbohydrates 29.46g 10% | Fiber 7.5g 30% | Sugar 5.74g | Protein 9.7g 19%

Vegan Potato and Mushroom Frittata

Ready in Time: 40 minutes | Servings: 4

Ingredients

1 lb waxy potatoes, cut into medium slices
1 large onion finely sliced
1 cup chickpea flour
1 cup dried mushrooms sliced
2 Tbsp fresh parsley finely chopped
Salt and ground black pepper to taste
4 Tbsp olive oil

Instructions

1. Cook potatoes in gently boiling water until tender or for about 18 to 20 minutes.
2. Drain in a colander and allow to cool a bit.
3. Place potatoes in a large bowl and add onion, chickpeas, mushrooms, parsley, and salt and pepper.
4. Mash with the fork, and then knead the mixture with your hand until combined well.
5. Heat oil into large frying skillet and add the potato mixture; cook for about 6 to 8 minutes over medium heat.
6. Gently flip it over, and cook from the other side for about 3 minutes.
7. Remove from skillet and place on a plate to cool down.
8. Cut into slices and store in an airtight container; keep refrigerated up to 3 to 4 days.

Nutrition Facts

Percent daily values based on the Reference Daily Intake (RDI) for a 2000 calorie diet.

Amount Per Serving

Calories 226 | Calories From Fat (59%) 133.24 | Total Fat 15.16g 23% | Saturated Fat 2.05g 10% | Cholesterol 0mg 0% | Sodium 19.21mg <1% | Potassium 328.12mg 9% | Total Carbohydrates 17.11g 6% | Fiber 3.35g 13% | Sugar 4.35g | Protein 6g 12%

DINNER

Artichoke Hearths with Brown Rice

Preparation Time: 40 minutes | Servings: 4

Ingredients

1 cup of avocado oil (or sesame oil)

10 canned artichoke hearts, drained and chopped

1 cup cauliflower (divided into florets)

1 cup of brown rice

3 cups of vegetable broth

2 Tbsp of fresh parsley finely chopped

2 Tbsp fresh dill finely chopped

2 Tbsp lemon juice freshly squeezed

salt and ground pepper to taste

Instructions

1. Heat oil in a large pot over medium-high heat.
2. Add artichoke hearts and sauté for 5 minutes.
3. Add the cauliflower and sprinkle with the pinch of the salt and pepper; stir for two minutes.
4. Add all remaining ingredients and give a good stir.
5. Bring to a boil and reduce heat to medium.
6. Cover and cook for 25 minutes.
7. Taste and adjust seasonings.
8. Allow to cool down completely.
9. Store in a large airtight container and keep refrigerated up to 4 to 5 days.
10. To reheat, place the rice and artichokes into a heatproof dish and add little water or broth; cover and microwave on HIGH for approximately 1 to 2 minutes.

Nutrition Facts

Percent daily values based on the Reference Daily Intake (RDI) for a 2000 calorie diet.

Amount Per Serving

Calories 581.35 | Calories From Fat (45%) 263.17 | Total Fat 29.81g 46% | Saturated Fat 3.69g 18% | Cholesterol 1.23mg <1% | Sodium 1056mg 44% | Potassium 932.39mg 27% | Total Carbohydrates 72.6g 24% | Fiber 11.35g 45% | Sugar 0.69g | Protein 12.69g 25%

Baked Sweet Potato with Green Beans

Ready in Time: 1 hour and 10 minutes | Servings: 5

Ingredients

2 lbs sweet potatoes cut into cubes
1 tsp pumpkin pie spice
1/3 cup olive oil
3/4 lb canned green beans, drained
1 cup mushrooms (chopped fine)
1 1/2 cups of water
Salt and ground black pepper to taste

Instructions

1. Preheat oven to 350 F.
2. Grease 9-inch baking dish; set aside.
3. Blend the sweet potato cubes, oil, and pumpkin pie spice in a large bowl.
4. Cover and let it sit for about 5 minutes or until smooth.
5. Arrange the sweet potato mixture over the prepared baking dish, and cover with the green beans mixture.
6. Bake for about 1 hour or until sweet potato is soft.
7. Adjust seasonings and allow to cool completely.
8. Store in an airtight container and keep refrigerated up to 4 days.

Nutrition Facts

Percent daily values based on the Reference Daily Intake (RDI) for a 2000 calorie diet.

Amount Per Serving

Calories 158.78 | Calories From Fat (82%) 129.44 | Total Fat 14.65g 23% | Saturated Fat 2g 10% | Cholesterol 0mg 0% | Sodium 6.19mg <1% | Potassium 192.27mg 5% | Total Carbohydrates 6g 2% | Fiber 2.04g 8% | Sugar 2g | Protein 1.64g 3%

Beans and Cauliflower Soup

Ready in Time: 25 minutes | Servings: 6

Ingredients

1/4 cup olive oil

1 large onion cut in chunks

2 cloves garlic finely chopped

salt and ground pepper, to taste

2 can (11 oz) white beans

2 cups cauliflower

2 Tbsp chopped parsley

3 sprigs thyme

pepper

3 1/2 cups vegetable broth

Instructions

1. Heat oil in a large pot over medium-high heat.

2. Sauté the onion and garlic with a pinch of salt until soft and translucent.

3. Add white beans and stir for two minutes.

4. Add cauliflower and stir for one minute.

5. Add all remaining ingredients and stir for one minute.

6. Reduce heat to medium, cover, and cook for 10 minutes.

7. Remove the bean soup in a blender; blend until smooth.

8. Store in an airtight container in the fridge up to 5 days or freeze up to two months.

Nutrition Facts

Percent daily values based on the Reference Daily Intake (RDI) for a 2000 calorie diet.

Amount Per Serving

Calories 463.8 | Calories From Fat (23%) 107.56 | Total Fat 12.19g 19% | Saturated Fat 2g 10% | Cholesterol 2.88mg <1% | Sodium 637.61mg 27% | Potassium 1941mg 55% | Total Carbohydrates 66.48g 22% | Fiber 15.16g 61% | Sugar 3.47g | Protein 25.43g 51%

Beans, Sesame and Pine Nuts Puree

Ready in Time: 20 minutes | Servings: 4

Ingredients

1 lb broad beans

2 cups boiling water

salt and ground black pepper to taste

1/3 cup sesame or avocado oil

1 tsp garlic powder

1/4 cup roasted pine nuts

1 Tbsp sesame seeds

1 Tbsp lemon juice, freshly squeezed

Instructions

1. Boil beans in a large pot for 2 minutes, throw water, and rinse them.

2. Add fresh water, a little salt, and boil broad beans for about 7 to 8 minutes.

3. Transfer broad beans into a high-speed blender along with all remaining ingredients blend until soft.

4. Taste and adjust seasonings.

5. Store in an airtight container and ref up to 5 days.

Nutrition Facts

Percent daily values based on the Reference Daily Intake (RDI) for a 2000 calorie diet.

Amount Per Serving

Calories 323.6 | Calories From Fat (66%) 214.7 | Total Fat 24.64g 38% | Saturated Fat 3.04g 15% | Cholesterol 0mg 0% | Sodium 106.16mg 4% | Potassium 458.62mg 13% | Total Carbohydrates 23.15g 8% | Fiber 0.52g 2% | Sugar 0.73g | Protein 10.38g 21%

Beluga Lentils and Tofu 'Meatballs'

Ready in Time: 1 hour and 25 minutes | Servings: 3

Ingredients

1 cup black lentils uncooked

1 tsp fennel seed

1 cup quinoa (uncooked

Kosher salt and ground black pepper to taste

1 tsp granulated garlic

1/4 cup fresh cilantro finely chopped

6 oz extra- firm tofu, pressed down, patted dry and cut into tiny cubes

2 Tbs olive oil

Instructions

1. Heat water (about 3 cups) over high heat and add lentils, fennel, and a pinch of salt and pepper.
2. Bring lentils to a boil, and turn heat medium-low.
3. Cover and cook for about 25 minutes.
4. When ready, rinse, and drain well.
5. In a small pot, add one cup of water and bring quinoa to boil.
6. Cover and simmer for 15 minutes; rinse and drain.
7. Preheat oven to 400 F.
8. Line a baking sheet with parchment paper; set aside.
9. Combine lentils and quinoa in a food processor.
10. Add all remaining ingredients, season generously with the salt and pepper; pulse until the texture of coarse sand.
11. Shape the mixture into 'meat' balls.
12. Place lentil balls onto a prepared baking sheet, and bake for 20 to 25 minutes.
13. Remove from the oven, and allow to cool completely.
14. Store in an airtight container in the fridge for up to 5 days.
15. Or, pack 'meatballs' in freezer bags and keep in freezer up to 3 months.

Nutrition Facts

Percent daily values based on the Reference Daily Intake (RDI) for a 2000 calorie diet.

Amount Per Serving

Calories 468.29 | Calories From Fat (28%) 129.82 | Total Fat 14.84g 23% | Saturated Fat 1.86g 9% | Cholesterol 0mg 0% | Sodium 13.4mg <1% | Potassium 895.34mg 26% | Total Carbohydrates 59g 20% | Fiber 22.23g 89% | Sugar 1.61g | Protein 26.5g 53%

Black Eyed Beans with Spinach

Ready in Time: 40 minutes | Servings: 6

Ingredients

1/2 lb black-eyed peas
1/2 cup olive oil
1 carrot, sliced 1" thick
2 green onions (only white parts)
2 stalks of celery
1 lb fresh spinach roughly chopped
1 lemon, juiced
1 tsp garlic powder
salt and black pepper, freshly ground
1/2 cup tomato juice
1 cup vegetable broth

Instructions

1. Rinse the beans and place them in your Instant Pot.
2. Add all remaining ingredients and stir well.
3. Lock lid into place and set on the MANUAL setting high pressure for 25 minutes.
4. Release pressure naturally for 10 minutes and quick-release remaining pressure.
5. Taste and adjust seasonings to taste.
6. Serve hot.
7. Allow cooling completely.
8. Keep refrigerated in an airtight container up to 4 to 5 days.

Nutrition Facts

Percent daily values based on the Reference Daily Intake (RDI) for a 2000 calorie diet.

Amount Per Serving

Calories 363 | Calories From Fat (47%) 172.1 | Total Fat 19.51g 30% | Saturated Fat 2.77g 14% | Cholesterol 0.41mg <1% | Sodium 361.9mg 15% | Potassium 1057.24mg 30% | Total Carbohydrates 37.19g 12% | Fiber 13.26g 53% | Sugar 6.6g | Protein 13.33g 27%

Eggplants with Peppercorn - Tamari Sauce

Ready in Time: 35 minutes | Servings: 6

Ingredients

1 1/2 lbs eggplants cut into 4 x 10-inch pieces
pinch of salt
1/3 cup peanut oil
4 cloves garlic chopped
2 tsp fresh ginger, finely minced
5 to 6 dried red chilies
1/2 cup of lukewarm water
Peppercorn - Tamari Sauce
1 tsp peppercorns
1/3 cup of tamari sauce
1 tsp chili flakes
2 Tbsp sesame oil
1 Tbsp vinegar (any)
2 Tbsp of dark honey
1/4 tsp of cinnamon

Instructions

1. Peal, clean, and sprinkle eggplant pieces with the salt, and brush with the oil.
2. Heat the peanut oil in a wok or large frying skillet over medium-high heat.
3. Sauté garlic with the pinch of salt for about 3 to 4 minutes.
4. Add eggplants, ginger, and red chilies, and stir for two minutes.
5. Pour water, reduce heat to medium-low, cover, and cook for 10 minutes.
6. In the meantime, prepare the sauce; combine all sauce ingredients in a bowl.
7. Pour sauce into wok/frying skillet, stir, and cook for a further 2 to 3 minutes.
8. Remove from the heat, and allow it to cool completely.
9. Store in an airtight container in the fridge for up to 4 to 5 days.

Nutrition Facts

Percent daily values based on the Reference Daily Intake (RDI) for a 2000 calorie diet.

Amount Per Serving

Calories 252.6 | Calories From Fat (60%) 150.5 | Total Fat 17.06g 26% | Saturated Fat 2.76g 14% | Cholesterol 0mg 0% | Sodium 1152.58mg 53% | Potassium 614.58mg 18% | Total Carbohydrates 24.65g 8% | Fiber 4.36g 17% | Sugar 9.15g | Protein 5g 10%

Garlic Black Beans and Rice Stew

Ready in Time: 40 minutes | Servings: 5

Ingredients

4 Tbsp of sesame oil

6 cloves minced garlic

Salt and Freshly-ground black pepper to taste

2 cups long-grain rice

1 can of black beans drained

4 cups vegetable broth

1/2 cup of soy sauce

1/2 cup of tomato sauce or crushed tomatoes

Instructions

1. Heat oil in a large skillet over medium-high heat; saute the garlic with a pinch of salt and pepper, constantly stirring, for about 3 to 4 minutes.
2. Add the black beans and rice, and stir for further two minutes.
3. Add the broth, soy sauce, and tomato sauce; stir for one minute.
4. Bring to a boil, reduce heat to medium, cover, and cook for 20 to 25 minutes.
5. Remove from the heat, and adjust the salt and pepper.
6. Store in an airtight container and keep refrigerated up to 4 to 5 days.

Nutrition Facts

Percent daily values based on the Reference Daily Intake (RDI) for a 2000 calorie diet.

Amount Per Serving

Calories 486 | Calories From Fat (27%) 130.35 | Total Fat 14.6g 23% | Saturated Fat 2.41g 12% | Cholesterol 1.7mg <1% | Sodium 1446.61mg 62% | Potassium 704.91mg 20% | Total Carbohydrates 73.3g 24% | Fiber 9.91g 40% | Sugar 1.53g | Protein 15.7g 31%

Gigante Beans and Tomatoes Stew

Ready in Time: 1 hour and 10 minutes | Servings: 6

Ingredients

3/4 lbs Gigante Beans soaked overnight

1/2 cup of olive oil

1 large onion, finely chopped

3 cloves garlic finely sliced

salt and freshly ground pepper

3/4 lb grated tomatoes or canned peeled tomatoes

1/2 bunch of parsley, finely chopped

1/2 Tbsp fresh thyme

1/2 tsp crushed red pepper flakes

2 cups of vegetable broth

2 cups of water

Instructions

1. Soak the Gigante beans covered in a warm place.
2. Press the SAUTÉ button on your Instant Pot and heat the oil.
3. Sauté the onion and garlic with a pinch of salt and pepper until soft.
4. Add grated tomatoes and soaked beans; stir for two minutes.
5. Add parsley, thyme, and red flakes; stir.
6. Add water and broth, and give a good stir.
7. Lock lid into place and set on the MANUAL setting high pressure for 50 minutes.
8. Once the pot beeps finished, use the Naturally release for 10 minutes and quick-release remaining pressure.
9. Taste and adjust the salt and pepper to taste.
10. Store in an airtight container, and keep refrigerated up to 4 to 5 days or keep frozen in a freezer-bags up to 4 to 5 months.

Nutrition Facts

Percent daily values based on the Reference Daily Intake (RDI) for a 2000 calorie diet.

Amount Per Serving

Calories 428,43 | Calories From Fat (41%) 175,92 | Total Fat 19.92g 31% | Saturated Fat 2.93g 15% | Cholesterol 0.82mg <1% | Sodium 558.12mg 23% | Potassium 1349.68mg 39% | Total Carbohydrates 48.61g 16% | Fiber 11g 44% | Sugar 3.61g | Protein 16.53g 34%

Greek Ratatouille

Ready in Time: 25 minutes | Servings: 4

Ingredients

3/4 of olive oil

1 onion finely diced

2 cloves garlic finely sliced

Salt and ground pepper to taste

2 potatoes cut into cubes

1 eggplant cut into cubes

1 lb zucchini cut into rings

1 pepper (red-green) sliced

2 Tbs fresh chopped mint, basil, and parsley

1 can (11 oz) of crushed tomatoes

1 tsp tomato paste

1 cup of water

1 vegetable bouillon cube of 1 cup of vegetable broth

Instructions

1. Pour oil to the inner stainless steel pot in the Instant Pot.
2. Turn on the Instant Pot and press the SAUTÉ button.
3. When the word "HOT" appears on display, sauté the onion and garlic with a pinch of the salt and pepper for about 3 to 4 minutes.
4. Add potato and eggplant cubes and stir for one minute.
5. Add zucchini and pepper and stir for one minute.
6. Add fresh chopped mint, basil and parsley, and stir well.
7. Add crushed tomatoes, tomato paste, water, and vegetable bouillon cube or one cup of vegetable broth; stir well.
8. Lock lid into place and set on the MANUAL setting high pressure for 12 minutes.
9. Use Quick Release - turn the valve from sealing to venting to release the pressure.
10. Stir, taste and adjust the salt and pepper to taste.
11. Store in an airtight container in the fridge for up to 4 days.

Nutrition Facts

Percent daily values based on the Reference Daily Intake (RDI) for a 2000 calorie diet.

Amount Per Serving

Calories 184.64 | Calories From Fat (35%) 65.1 | Total Fat 7.39g 11% | Saturated Fat 1.1g 5% | Cholesterol 0mg 0% | Sodium 190.2mg 8% | Potassium 961.61mg 27% | Total Carbohydrates 27.4g 9% | Fiber 4.9g 20% | Sugar 7.73g | Protein 4.61g 9%

Mediterranean Pie Stuffed with Black Olives

Ready in Time: 1 hour and 5 minutes | Servings: 10

Ingredients

For dough

3 1/2 cup of flour all-purposes

2 1 tsp baking soda

1 1/3 cups of olive oil

1 1/4 cups of orange juice

For stuffing

4 Tbsp of olive oil

2 large onions, finely chopped

3 cups of black olives pitted

3 tsp of fresh mint finely chopped

1 tsp sesame seeds toasted

1 tsp cumin seeds, crushed

Instructions

1. Preheat oven to 360 F.
2. Prepare and grease a round baking pan.
3. Combine the flour with the baking powder in a large bowl.
4. Whisk the olive oil and orange juice into a large bowl; stir well.
5. Combine the flour with the oil mixture, and knead well until get a smooth and light dough.
6. Divide dough into 2 sheets.
7. Heat the oil in a frying skillet and sauté onion until translucent; add olives and fresh chopped mint.
8. Stir and cook for about 3 minutes.
9. Place one sheet of dough into a prepared baking dish and spread the filling; sprinkle with sesame seeds and cumin.
10. Cover the mixture with the second sheet and gently chop the pie into pieces.
11. Bake for 45 minutes or until golden brown.
12. Remove from the oven, and let it sit until cool down completely.
13. Store in an airtight container and keep refrigerated up to 4 to 5 days or freeze your pie for up to one month.

Nutrition Facts

Percent daily values based on the Reference Daily Intake (RDI) for a 2000 calorie diet.

Amount Per Serving

Calories 426.55 | Calories From Fat (55%) 232.85 | Total Fat 26.53g 41% | Saturated Fat 3.64g 18% | Cholesterol 0mg 0% | Sodium 475.5mg 20% | Potassium 169.7mg 5% | Total Carbohydrates 42.64g 14% | Fiber 3.14g 13% | Sugar 4.28g | Protein 5.43g 11%

Penne with Lemony Asparagus

Ready in Time: 30 minutes | Servings: 2

Ingredients

8 oz pasta (of your preference)

2 cups sliced asparagus

4 Tbs olive oil

1/2 cup green onions, chopped

2 cloves garlic minced

2 Tbsp fresh lemon juice

2 tsp lemon rind

salt and ground black pepper to taste

Instructions

1. Cook pasta according to package directions.

2. Add asparagus to pasta during the last 3 minutes of cooking time; drain.

3. Heat oil in a large frying skillet over medium-high heat.

4. Sauté green onions and garlic with a pinch of salt for about 4 to 5 minutes.

5. Add pasta, asparagus, lemon juice, lemon rind, and the salt and pepper to taste.

6. Stir and cook for two minutes.

7. Taste and adjust the salt.

8. Store pasta in an airtight container in the fridge for up to 4 days.

Nutrition Facts

Percent daily values based on the Reference Daily Intake (RDI) for a 2000 calorie diet.

Amount Per Serving

Calories 703.14 | Calories From Fat (37%) 257.34 | Total Fat 29g 45% | Saturated Fat 4.05g 20% | Cholesterol 0mg 0% | Sodium 161.21mg 7% | Potassium 556.6mg 16% | Total Carbohydrates 94.12g 31% | Fiber 6.31g 25% | Sugar 3.64g | Protein 18.16g 36%

Quinoa with Vegetables Briam

Ready in Time: 35 minutes | Servings: 5

Ingredients

4 Tbs olive oil
1 onion finely sliced
2 cloves garlic finely sliced
1 green pepper, chopped
1 red bell pepper
Salt and ground pepper to taste
1 eggplant cut into slices
2 medium zucchini sliced
2 ripped tomatoes grated
1/2 cup quinoa
1 cup of vegetable broth

Instructions

1. Rinse quinoa in a fine-mesh sieve until water runs clear; set aside.
2. Heat oil n a non-stick frying skillet over medium-high heat.
3. Sauté the onion, garlic, peppers, eggplant, and zucchini with a pinch of salt and pepper.
4. Add grated tomato, stir well, cover, and simmer vegetables over medium heat for about 10 minutes.
5. Add quinoa and vegetable broth, stir well, and cook for further 10 to12 minutes or until any liquid is absorbed
6. Remove from the heat, taste, and adjust the salt and pepper to taste.
7. Store in an airtight container in the fridge for up to 4 to 5 days.
8. Or, transfer the quinoa mixture to a resealable freezer bag and keep in freezer up to 6 months.

Nutrition Facts

Percent daily values based on the Reference Daily Intake (RDI) for a 2000 calorie diet.

Amount Per Serving

Calories 262.62 | Calories From Fat (45%) 117.6 | Total Fat 13.31g 20% | Saturated Fat 1.94g 10% | Cholesterol 0.49mg <1% | Sodium 340.63mg 14% | Potassium 879.8mg 25% | Total Carbohydrates 31.84g 11% | Fiber 7.6g 32% | Sugar 8.6g | Protein 6.87g 14%

Roasted Brussels sprouts with Tofu

Ready in Time: 45 minutes | Servings: 4

Ingredients

1 1/2 lbs Brussels sprouts halved

1 block of extra - firm tofu drained and cut into cubes

Salt and pepper to taste

1/3 cup sesame oil

2 Tbsp soy sauce

2 Tbsp rice vinegar

1 tsp oregano

Instructions

1. Preheat oven to 350 F.
2. Clean and cut the Brussels sprouts in halves.
3. Place Brussels sprouts and tofu cubes in a large baking dish.
4. Season evenly with the salt and pepper.
5. Whisk oil, soy sauce, rice vinegar, oregano, and the salt and pepper in a small bowl.
6. Pour the sesame oil mixture evenly over the Brussels sprouts and tofu.
7. Bake for about 30 minutes.
8. Remove from the oven, and allow it to cool down completely.
9. Store in an airtight container for up to 4 days.

Nutrition Facts

Percent daily values based on the Reference Daily Intake (RDI) for a 2000 calorie diet.

Amount Per Serving

Calories 343.37 | Calories From Fat (64%) 220.27 | Total Fat 25.31g 39% | Saturated Fat 3.31g 17% | Cholesterol 0mg 0% | Sodium 464.24mg 19% | Potassium 884.57mg 25% | Total Carbohydrates 21.6g 7% | Fiber 7.14g 29% | Sugar 4.46g | Protein 17,45g 35%

Roasted Pepper Sauce

Ready in Time: 10 minutes | Servings: 6

Ingredients

1 glass roasted peppers, drained and chopped

4 Tbsp olive oil

1 cup finely chopped onion or shallot

3 cloves garlic minced

1/2 cup drained whole canned tomatoes

2 Tbsp chopped fresh parsley

Salt and freshly ground pepper, to taste

Instructions

1. Add all ingredients into a high-speed blender or food processor.

2. Blend until smooth.

3. Store your sauce in a tightly sealed jar or bottle, and keep refrigerated up to two weeks

4. Reheat sauce to be served warm over low heat.

Nutrition Facts

Percent daily values based on the Reference Daily Intake (RDI) for a 2000 calorie diet.

Amount Per Serving

Calories 114.32 | Calories From Fat (71%) 81.1 | Total Fat 9.19g 14% | Saturated Fat 1.27g 6% | Cholesterol 0mg 0% | Sodium 32.14mg 1% | Potassium 207.6mg 6% | Total Carbohydrates 8.15g 3% | Fiber 2.25g 9% | Sugar 1.63g | Protein 1.47g 2%

Simple Vegan Lasagna with Tofu

Ready in Time: 1 hour and 20 minutes | Servings: 8

Ingredients

For the lasagna:

8 whole vegan grain lasagna noodles

2 Tbs olive oil

1 cup sliced mushrooms

3/4 lb frozen spinach, thawed

1 cup frozen peas, thawed

6 cups marinara sauce

For the tofu spread:

1 1/4 lb extra firm tofu, drained and pressed

1 cup hummus

4 Tbs nutritional yeast

1 tsp garlic powder

1/4 cup fresh basil, finely chopped

Sea salt and ground black pepper

Instructions

1. Preheat oven to 350 F.
2. Place about 1 1/2 cups of marinara sauce in the bottom of a large baking dish; set aside.
3. Cook vegan noodles al dente; drain and rinse with cold water.
4. Heat oil in a large frying skillet over medium heat.
5. Add mushrooms and a pinch of salt and pepper; sauté for 3 to 4 minutes.
6. Add spinach and peas and sauté for further 4 to 5 minutes.
7. Remove pan from the heat.
8. Place drained tofu in a large bowl; crumble with hands.
9. Add hummus, nutritional yeast, basil, salt, and garlic powder.
10. Stir together with your hands until combined well.
11. Top 4 noodles in a prepared baking dish with marinara sauce.
12. Add half of the tofu mixture and half of the vegetable mixture.
13. Top with 1 1/2 cups of marinara sauce.
14. Repeat with more noodles, tofu mixture, and vegetables.
15. Finally, top with one last layer of noodles and all remaining sauce.
16. Sprinkle with nutritional yeast.
17. Cover with foil and bake for 30 minutes.
18. Remove from the oven and allow to cool completely.
19. Cut your lasagna and store in a large airtight container; keep refrigerated up to 4 to 5 days.
20. Or, place your lasagna into heavy-duty freezer bags, and freeze up to one month.

Nutrition Facts

Percent daily values based on the Reference Daily Intake (RDI) for a 2000 calorie diet.

Amount Per Serving

Calories 413.29 | Calories From Fat (29%) 119.48 | Total Fat 13.75g 21% | Saturated Fat 2.12g 11% | Cholesterol 2.57mg <1% | Sodium 750.94mg 31% | Potassium 825.36mg 24% | Total Carbohydrates 55.81g 19% | Fiber 8.6g 35% | Sugar 13g | Protein 19.61g 40%

Stuffed Bell Peppers with Rice and Pine Nuts

Ready in Time: 1 hour and 30 minutes | Servings: 8

Ingredients

8 bell peppers (green or red)
1 cup of olive oil
1 large onion finely diced
3 cloves garlic minced
1 large carrot grated
1 cup of rice
1 cup of fresh tomato juice
3 Tbsp semolina flour
Salt and ground pepper to taste
2 Tbsp fresh parsley finely chopped
1 Tbsp fresh basil finely chopped
1 cup pine nuts
1 cup raisins
juice of 2 tomatoes

Instructions

1. Cut the stems of papers and set aside.
2. Remove seeds from peppers and rinse well; set aside to drain.
3. Heat the half of oil in a large frying skillet and sauté the onion, garlic, rice, carrot on high heat.
4. Reduce the heat to moderate, add the tomato, semolina, and the salt and pepper; stir well and remove the pan from the heat.
5. Add the herbs, pine nuts, raisins to the mixture, and stir well.
6. Taste and adjust the salt and ground pepper to taste.
7. Preheat oven to 400 F.
8. Fill the peppers with the rice mixture and cover with their stems or tomato slices.
9. Place stuffed peppers into an oiled baking dish and pour with remaining olive oil and some tomato juice.
10. Bake for about 55 to 60 minutes.
11. Remove from the oven, and let it sit until cool completely.
12. Keep refrigerated in one or two airtight containers up to 4 to 5 days or freeze for up to a month.

Nutrition Facts

Percent daily values based on the Reference Daily Intake (RDI) for a 2000 calorie diet.

Amount Per Serving

Calories 426.48 | Calories From Fat (56%) 238.7 | Total Fat 27.38g 42% | Saturated Fat 3.29g 16% | Cholesterol 0mg 0% | Sodium 93mg 4% | Potassium 605.08mg 17% | Total Carbohydrates 43.86g 15% | Fiber 6.81g 27% | Sugar 12.55g | Protein 5.86g 12%

Sweet Red and Black Chili with Cinnamon

Ready in Time: 45 minutes | Servings: 6

Ingredients

4 Tbs of olive oil

1 onion finely diced

2 cloves garlic, chopped

1 red pepper cut into small cubes

Kosher salt and ground black pepper to taste

1 can (15 oz) red beans, cooked

1 can (11 oz) of black beans

1 can (11 oz) crushed tomatoes

2 tsp chili powder

1/4 tsp ground cinnamon

2 Tbsp fresh parsley finely chopped

2 cups of vegetable broth

Instructions

1. Press the SAUTÉ button on your Instant Pot.
2. When the word "hot" appears on display, add the oil and sauté the onion and garlic with a pinch of salt and pepper until soft; stir occasionally.
3. Add red pepper and stir for one minute.
4. Add red and black beans and stir for one minute.
5. Add all remaining ingredients and give a good stir.
6. Lock lid into place and set on the MANUAL setting high pressure for 20 minutes.
7. When the beep sounds, use the Natural pressure release for 15 minutes.
8. Taste and adjust salt and pepper to taste.
9. Store in an airtight container in the fridge for up to 5 days.
10. Or, let the chili cool a bit, then pack it in a freezer bag or Tupperware container and keep in freezer up to 3 months.

Nutrition Facts

Percent daily values based on the Reference Daily Intake (RDI) for a 2000 calorie diet.

Amount Per Serving

Calories 266.41 | Calories From Fat (34%) 90.97 | Total Fat 10.39g 16% | Saturated Fat 1.58g 8% | Cholesterol 0mg 0% | Sodium 464.62mg 19% | Potassium 686.1mg 20% | Total Carbohydrates 33.73g 11% | Fiber 11.23g 45% | Sugar 4.84g | Protein 12.1g 24%

Tuscan Kale with Tamari Sauce

Ready in Time: 15 minutes | Servings: 2

Ingredients

4 cups Tuscan kale

4 Tbsp sesame oil or olive oil

2 tsp Japanese sweet rice wine (or vinegar)

2 Tbsp Tamari sauce

Salt to taste

Instructions

1. Rinse well your kale and cut the bottom side of the stem.
2. Cut kale from top to bottom with the knife.
3. Heat oil in a wok/frying skillet over medium-high heat.
4. Cook kale for about 2 to 3 minutes, stirring frequently.
5. Pour cooking wine (or vinegar) and cook for further one minute.
6. Pour the tamari sauce, stir well and sprinkle with a pinch of salt
7. Cook for a further 2 to 3 minutes or until slightly wilted.
8. Allow cooling completely.
9. Store in an airtight container and keep refrigerated up to 3 to 4 days.

Nutrition Facts

Percent daily values based on the Reference Daily Intake (RDI) for a 2000 calorie diet.

Amount Per Serving

Calories 249.48 | Calories From Fat (96%) 238.3 | Total Fat 27g 42% | Saturated Fat 3.73g 19% | Cholesterol 0mg 0% | Sodium 1006mg 42% | Potassium 38.43mg 1% | Total Carbohydrates 1g <1% | Fiber 0.14g <1% | Sugar 0.31g | Protein 1.9g 4%

Yellow Noodles in Garlic - Hoisin Sauce

Ready in Time: 15 minutes | Servings: 3

Ingredients

20 oz yellow type noodles or spaghetti

Water, for boiling the noodles

Garlic - hoisin sauce

1/2 cup avocado oil

3 Tbsp minced garlic

2 Tbsp hoisin sauce

1 Tbs yellow mustard (without alcohol)

1 Tbs of granulated sugar

Instructions

1. Add yellow noodles into the boiling water and cook for 3 to 4 minutes or until al dente.
2. Transfer the noodles in a colander to drain; set aside.
3. Add all sauce ingredients into saucepan; stir over medium-high heat for about 3 minutes.
4. Transfer warm sauce into a large bowl.
5. Toss noodles into the sauce and toss to combine well.
6. Store in an airtight container and keep refrigerated up to 4 days.

Nutrition Facts

Percent daily values based on the Reference Daily Intake (RDI) for a 2000 calorie diet.

Amount Per Serving

Calories 897.59 | Calories From Fat (26%) 254.28 | Total Fat 28.93g 45% | Saturated Fat 3.55g 18% | Cholesterol 0.32mg <1% | Sodium 244.63mg 10% | Potassium 485.7mg 14% | Total Carbohydrates 154.2g 52% | Fiber 6.77g 27% | Sugar 12.32g | Protein 26.1g 52%

SNACKS

Banana and Peanut Butter Tortillas

Ready in Time: 15 minutes | Servings: 4

Ingredients

1/3 cup peanut butter
4 medium tortillas
2 large bananas sliced
3 Tbsp peanut oil
Pinch of Kosher salt
Pine Honey for serving (optional)

Instructions

1. Heat a non-stick frying skillet over medium heat.
2. Spread peanut butter over the tortilla.
3. Over half of tortilla arrange the banana slices, sprinkle with a pinch of salt, and top with the remaining tortilla, peanut butter side down.
4. Stick them together and then brush both sides lightly with peanut oil.
5. Place each tortilla in a hot frying pan and cook, flipping once, for about 2 minutes per side.
6. When ready, remove tortillas onto a plate and let cool completely.
7. Cut each tortilla into quarters; store in an airtight container and keep refrigerated up to 5 days.

Nutrition Facts

Percent daily values based on the Reference Daily Intake (RDI) for a 2000 calorie diet.

Amount Per Serving

Calories 371.59 | Calories From Fat (56%) 206.9 | Total Fat 24g 37% | Saturated Fat 3.7g 19% | Cholesterol 0mg 0% | Sodium 302.79mg 13% | Potassium 400.35mg 11% | Total Carbohydrates 34.11g 11% | Fiber 3.82g 15% | Sugar 9.81g | Protein 8.69g 18%

Barbecue Bean Dip (Instant Pot)

Ready in Time: 20 minutes | Servings: 8

Ingredients

1 can (15 oz) cannellini beans rinsed

1 can (6 oz) red beans rinsed and drained

1/2 cup onion finely diced

2 cloves garlic minced

4 Tbsp Barbecue sauce

1/2 cup tomato sauce

3/4 cup vegan ricotta or vegan brie

1 Tbsp fresh parsley chopped

table salt to taste

Instructions

1. Add all ingredients in your Instant Pot.
2. Lock lid into place and set on the MANUAL setting for 15 minutes.
3. When the timer beeps, press "Cancel" and carefully flip the Quick Release valve to let the pressure out.
4. Using an immersion blender, blend the mixture until soft.
5. Transfer dip into the container, and allow to cool down completely.
6. Keep refrigerated up to 5 days.

Nutrition Facts

Percent daily values based on the Reference Daily Intake (RDI) for a 2000 calorie diet.

Amount Per Serving

Calories 297.81 | Calories From Fat (7%) 21.84 | Total Fat 2.5g 4% | Saturated Fat 0.42g 2% | Cholesterol 0mg 0% | Sodium 233.63mg 10% | Potassium 1410.7mg 40% | Total Carbohydrates 50.69g 17% | Fiber 12.19g 49% | Sugar 3.7g | Protein 20.23g 40%

Breaded Cauliflower Florets

Ready in Time: 45 minutes | Servings: 6

Ingredients

1 large head of cauliflower

1 cup rice flour (besan or wheat flour)

1 tsp salt

3/4 tsp garlic powder

3/4 cup water

1 cup chili sauce

2 Tbsp plant butter (any) softened

Instructions

1. Preheat oven to 420 F.
2. Line a large baking sheet with parchment paper; set aside.
3. Rise, clean and cut cauliflower into florets; place in a large bowl.
4. In a separate bowl, combine the rice flour, salt, garlic powder, and water; stir well.
5. Pour the mixture evenly over the cauliflower florets and toss to combine well.
6. Place cauliflower on a prepared baking sheet in a single layer.
7. Place in oven and bake for 15 minutes.
8. In a bowl, whisk together hot sauce and vegetable butter.
9. Transfer the cauliflower to a large bowl.
10. Pour the sauce evenly over cauliflower pieces.
11. Transfer the cauliflower back on the baking sheet and for further 15 minutes.
12. Remove the cauliflower from the oven and set aside to cool down.
13. Refrigerate the cauliflower in an airtight container up to 4 days.

Nutrition Facts

Percent daily values based on the Reference Daily Intake (RDI) for a 2000 calorie diet.

Amount Per Serving

Calories 98.51 | Calories From Fat (29%) 28.58 | Total Fat 3.41g 5% | Saturated Fat 0.31g 2% | Cholesterol 0mg 0% | Sodium 732.57mg 31% | Potassium 375.9mg 11% | Total Carbohydrates 14.43g 5% | Fiber 2.88g 12% | Sugar 2.4g | Protein 4.24g 8%

Coconut- Berry Cream with Turmeric

Ready in Time: 10 minutes | Servings: 4

Ingredients

1 1/2 cups coconut milk canned

1 Tbsp coconut cream softened

1 cup of frozen berries (blueberries, bilberries, raspberries)

1 cup fresh pineapple cut into pieces

1 small banana sliced (frozen or fresh)

1/2 tsp turmeric, freshly grated

2 to 3 Tbsp coconut palm sugar (or granulated sugar)

Instructions

1. Place all ingredients in your fast-speed blender.

2. Blend until smooth and combined well.

3. Taste and adjust sugar to taste.

4. Keep refrigerated in a glass container or jar for up to 5 days.

Nutrition Facts

Percent daily values based on the Reference Daily Intake (RDI) for a 2000 calorie diet.

Amount Per Serving

Calories 252.46 | Calories From Fat (61%) 154.42 | Total Fat 18.5g 28% | Saturated Fat 16.16g 81% | Cholesterol 0mg 0% | Sodium 12.17mg <1% | Potassium 358mg 10% | Total Carbohydrates 24.32g 8% | Fiber 2.19g 9% | Sugar 14.42g | Protein 2.51g 5%

Creamy Eggplant-Flax Dip

Ready in Time: 20 minutes | Servings: 10

Ingredients

2 eggplants peeled and cut into pieces
1 small onion chopped into small dices
3 Tbsp olive oil
2 clove garlic minced or mashed
1/3 cup of flaxseed flour
1 cup vegetable broth
salt and ground black pepper t to taste
1 cup of vegan mayonnaise

Instructions

1. Peel, rinse and cut eggplant lengthwise into pieces.
2. Add all ingredients (except Mayo) in your Instant Pot; give a good stir.
3. Lock lid into place and set on the MANUAL setting high pressure for 10 minutes.
4. When the beep sounds, quick release the pressure by pressing Cancel, and twisting the steam handle to the Venting position.
5. Remove the mixture into your blender or food processor.
6. Add vegan mayonnaise, and season with the salt and pepper; stir until smooth and creamy.
7. Allow to cool completely, and keep refrigerated in a sealed container up to 5 days.

Nutrition Facts

Percent daily values based on the Reference Daily Intake (RDI) for a 2000 calorie diet.

Amount Per Serving

Calories 223.81 | Calories From Fat (83%) 184.79 | Total Fat 19g 29% | Saturated Fat 1.48g 7% | Cholesterol 0.25mg <1% | Sodium 277.11mg 12% | Potassium 269.6mg 8% | Total Carbohydrates 9.19g 3% | Fiber 3.65g 15% | Sugar 2.68g | Protein 1.69g 3%

Energy Carob Strawberry Bars

Preparation Time: 20 minutes | Servings: 8

Ingredients

1 cup dried dates soaked
1/4 cup carob powder
1/2 cup frozen strawberries
2 scoops vegan protein powder (e.g., chia, soy or hemp)
1/2 cup walnuts chopped
1/4 cup ground flaxseed
1/4 cup sunflower seeds
1/2 tsp lemon zest
1 tsp fresh lemon juice
Sea salt to taste

Instructions

1. Add all ingredients into your food processor.
2. Process until smooth and combined well.
3. Pour the mixture onto a lined baking tray; flat the surface with a knife or spatula.
4. Refrigerate for several hours (at least 4 hours).
5. Remove the mixture from the fridge and cut into bars.
6. Wrap each bar in plastic sheets, and store in an airtight container.
7. Keep refrigerated up to 3 to 4 weeks.

Nutrition Facts

Percent daily values based on the Reference Daily Intake (RDI) for a 2000 calorie diet.

Amount Per Serving

Calories 244 | Calories From Fat (52%) 126.24 | Total Fat 14.63g 23% | Saturated Fat 1.39g 7% | Cholesterol 1.16mg <1% | Sodium 41.6mg 2% | Potassium 301.84mg 9% | Total Carbohydrates 26.6g 9% | Fiber 3.81g 15% | Sugar 15.36g | Protein 5.12g 10%

Fragrant Spiced Olives

Ready in Time: 10 minutes | Servings: 4

Ingredients

1 tsp coriander seeds crushed

1 Tbsp water

1/2 cup extra-virgin olive oil

3 tsp orange zest

2 tsp garlic finely chopped

1/4 tsp crushed red pepper flakes

2 cups olives pitted (black, green or Kalamata)

1 tsp allspice (ground)

Instructions

1. Add crushed coriander seeds and water into a 1-quart saucepan and cook over medium heat, stirring, for about 1 minute.
2. Add in the olive oil, orange zest, garlic, and red pepper flakes; stir for one minute.
3. Add olives and allspice.
4. Warm your olives, often stirring, about two minutes.
5. Transfer olives to a bowl with liquids, and allow to cool completely.
6. Place olives in an airtight container or jar and keep refrigerated up to one week.

Nutrition Facts

Percent daily values based on the Reference Daily Intake (RDI) for a 2000 calorie diet.

Amount Per Serving

Calories 341.27 | Calories From Fat (92%) 314.6 | Total Fat 35.9g 55% | Saturated Fat 4.9g 24% | Cholesterol 0mg 0% | Sodium 732.71mg 31% | Potassium 26.43mg <1% | Total Carbohydrates 6.57g 2% | Fiber 3.15g 13% | Sugar 0.01g | Protein 1g 2%

Fried Chickpeas Cashew Fritters

Ready in Time: 25 minutes | Servings: 2

Ingredients

1/2 cup cashew halves soaked
1 cup chickpea flour
1/4 tsp turmeric
1/2 tsp red chili powder
1/4 tsp garlic paste
a pinch of baking soda
Salt to taste
2 Tbsp olive oil
water to knead
olive or sesame oil for frying

Instructions

1. Add all ingredients in a food processor; process until combined well.
2. Heat oil in a large non-stick frying skillet.
3. Shape the batter into fritters flatten into little rounds.
4. Fry for about 2 to 3 minutes per side, turning once, or until golden brown.
5. Using a slotted spoon drain onto paper towels., and let sit until cool completely.
6. Store fritters in an airtight container in a dark and cold place for up to one week.
7. Or, refrigerate fritters up to two months.

Nutrition Facts

Percent daily values based on the Reference Daily Intake (RDI) for a 2000 calorie diet.

Amount Per Serving

Calories 576.39 | Calories From Fat (62%) 358.54 | Total Fat 41.58g 64% | Saturated Fat 6.25g 31% | Cholesterol 0mg 0% | Sodium 820.9mg 34% | Potassium 602.94mg 17% | Total Carbohydrates 38.31g 13% | Fiber 6.3g 25% | Sugar 6.6g | Protein 15.7g 32%

Ginger-Turmeric Butternut Squash Chips

Ready in Time: 1 hour and 45 minutes | Servings: 4

Ingredients

1 lb butternut squash cut into 1/8 inch strips
4 Tbsp olive oil
1 tsp ground ginger
1/2 tsp turmeric
1 tsp cinnamon
1/4 tsp nutmeg
pinch salt
Maple syrup for serving (optional)

Instructions

1. Preheat oven to 250 F.
2. Line a baking sheet with parchment paper; set aside.
3. Place the butternut squash strips in a bowl.
4. In a separate bowl, combine all remaining ingredients.
5. Pour the mixture evenly over the butternut squash strips; lightly stir to combine well.
6. Place the butternut slices close to each other on a prepared baking sheet.
7. Bake until crispy or about 90 minutes.
8. When done, let them cool down and store in an air-tight container in the fridge for up to a week.

Nutrition Facts

Percent daily values based on the Reference Daily Intake (RDI) for a 2000 calorie diet.

Amount Per Serving

Calories 171.16 | Calories From Fat (69%) 118.89 | Total Fat 13.8g 21% | Saturated Fat 11.83g 59% | Cholesterol 0mg 0% | Sodium 4.76mg <1% | Potassium 410mg 12% | Total Carbohydrates 13.85g 5% | Fiber 2.54g 10% | Sugar 2.6g | Protein 1.19g 2%

Homemade Coconut - Vanilla Popcorn

Ready in Time: 25 minutes | Servings: 4

Ingredients

1 cup of unpopped popcorn kernels

3 Tbsp coconut oil melted

2 Tbsp ground almonds

2 tsp pure vanilla extract

2 Tbsp water

Instructions

1. Preheat oven to 350 F.
2. Pop your corn kernels in an air popper or use a microwave oven.
3. Whisk all remaining ingredients in a bowl.
4. Place popcorn in a large and deep bowl, and pour with the coconut oil mixture.
5. Pack the popcorn into an airtight container, and keep on room temperature up to 10 days.

Nutrition Facts

Percent daily values based on the Reference Daily Intake (RDI) for a 2000 calorie diet.

Amount Per Serving

Calories 307.13 | Calories From Fat (41%) 126.13 | Total Fat 14.6g 22% | Saturated Fat 9.32g 47% | Cholesterol 0mg 0% | Sodium 4.04mg <1% | Potassium 170.9mg 5% | Total Carbohydrates 37.74g 13% | Fiber 6.82g 27% | Sugar 0.93g | Protein 6.34g 13%

Oat Biscuits with Seeds

Ready in Time: 30 minutes | Yield: 16 biscuits | Servings: 4

Ingredients

4 Tbsp coconut butter melted

1/2 cup of oatmeal

1/2 cup almond flour

1 tsp baking soda

2 Tbsp sesame seeds

2 tsp poppy seeds

5 to 6 Tbsp of warm water

Instructions

1. Heat oven to 360 F.
2. Grease a large baking sheet and sprinkle with the flour; set aside.
3. Add all ingredients into a bowl, and stir well combine to make a firm dough.
4. Transfer dough onto a lightly floured surface and roll out until getting a thick dough.
5. Cut into small squares and place onto a prepared baking sheet.
6. Bake for about 13 to15 minutes.
7. Remove from the oven, and allow to cool completely.
8. Place biscuits in an airtight container and keep at room temperature up to 2 weeks.

Nutrition Facts

Percent daily values based on the Reference Daily Intake (RDI) for a 2000 calorie diet.

Amount Per Serving

Calories 229.21 | Calories From Fat (68%) 155.1 | Total Fat 17.76g 27% | Saturated Fat 12.38g 62% | Cholesterol 0mg 0% | Sodium 317.12mg 13% | Potassium 115.24mg 3% | Total Carbohydrates 14.37g 5% | Fiber 2.87g 11% | Sugar 0.06g | Protein 4.34g 9%

Olive Crackers

Preparation Time: 35 minutes | Servings: 16

Ingredients

3/4 cup of flour all-purposes

1 tsp yeast

pinch of salt

1/2 cup of olive oil

1 tsp garlic powder

1/2 cup almond milk

12 black olives finely chopped

1 tsp oregano

2 Tbsp nut cheese (any) crumbled

Instructions

1. Preheat oven to 400 F.
2. Line a baking sheet with parchment paper; set aside.
3. Combine flour, yeast, salt, garlic powder, and almond milk.
4. Stir with a wooden spoon until combined well.
5. Knead the dough by hand until smooth.
6. Form the dough into a ball, wrap in cling film and refrigerate for 2 hours.
7. Take the dough out, fold chopped olives, oregano, and nut cheese; knead lightly.
8. Dust the working surface with flour and roll the dough.
9. Cut the crackers, and arrange on a prepared baking sheet.
10. Bake for 12 to 15 minutes or until golden brown.
11. Store in a sealed container and keep refrigerated for one week.

Nutrition Facts

Percent daily values based on the Reference Daily Intake (RDI) for a 2000 calorie diet.

Amount Per Serving

Calories 138.3 | Calories From Fat (75%) 103.18 | Total Fat 11.86g 18% | Saturated Fat 1.57g 8% | Cholesterol 0mg 0% | Sodium 373.41mg 16% | Potassium 23.3mg <1% | Total Carbohydrates 7.63g 3% | Fiber 1.76g 7% | Sugar 0.08g | Protein 1.27g 3%

Oven-baked Kale-Cashews Chips

Inactive Time: 1 hour | Total Time: 2 hours and 40 minutes | Servings: 6

Instructions

1 cup cashews chopped (soaked)

1 lb fresh kale leaves cut in large pieces

3 Tbsp lemon juice

2 Tbsp water

3 cloves garlic minced

1/3 cup of olive oil

1 tsp red sweet paprika

Pinch of salt

Instructions

1. Soak the cashews in water for at least one hour; drain.
2. Preheat the oven to 200 F.
3. Line a large baking sheet with a foil or parchment paper; set aside.
4. Wash and rinse kale thoroughly and tear the kale in large pieces.
5. Add drained cashews with lemon juice, water, garlic, olive oil, and red paprika in a blender.
6. Blend on HIGH until smooth and combined well.
7. In a large bowl, toss the cashews sauce with kale to combine well
8. Spread the kale leaves evenly on a prepared baking sheet.
9. Bake for 2 1/2 hours, flipping twice.
10. Remove kale chips and allow them to cool down completely.
11. Place kale chips in a zip lock bag and keep refrigerated.

Nutrition Facts

Percent daily values based on the Reference Daily Intake (RDI) for a 2000 calorie diet.

Amount Per Serving

Calories 200.46 | Calories From Fat (73%) 145.57 | Total Fat 16.71g 26% | Saturated Fat 2.55g 13% | Cholesterol 0mg 0% | Sodium 133.25mg 6% | Potassium 422.7mg 12% | Total Carbohydrates 11.2g 4% | Fiber 2g 8% | Sugar 1.13g | Protein 4.2g 8%

Pesto Dip with Nuts

Ready in Time: 10 minutes | Servings: 4

Ingredients

1 cup fresh basil leaves, chopped

2 cups zucchini, peeled and chopped

2 cloves garlic minced

1 cup walnuts soaked

1 cup lemon juice from 2 lemons, freshly squeezed

1/2 tsp cumin

Sea salt and black pepper to taste

Instructions

1. Add all ingredients in a high-speed blender; blend until completely smooth.
2. Taste and adjust seasonings to taste.
3. Keep refrigerated in a sealed glass jar for up to one week.

Nutrition Facts

Percent daily values based on the Reference Daily Intake (RDI) for a 2000 calorie diet.

Amount Per Serving

Calories 67.38 | Calories From Fat (64%) 43 | Total Fat 5.14g 8% | Saturated Fat 0.52g 3% | Cholesterol 0mg 0% | Sodium 6.38mg <1% | Potassium 251.75mg 7% | Total Carbohydrates 4.88g 2% | Fiber 1.38g 6% | Sugar 2.18g | Protein 2.39g 5%

Protein Almonds and Carrots Patties

Ready in Time: 15 minutes | Servings: 3

Ingredients

1 cup ground almonds

1/2 cup ground flaxseed

2 large carrots, shredded

2 Tbsp lemon juice, freshly squeezed

3 cloves garlic, finely minced

1 pinch salt and black pepper

3 Tbsp garlic-infused olive oil (or extra-virgin olive oil)

1 scoop vegan protein powder (pea or soy protein)

1 cup water for Instant Pot

Instructions

1. Place all ingredients in a blender and blend until combined well.
2. Shape the mixtures into two or three patties.
3. Pour water to the inner steel pot in the Instant Pot, and place the steamer basket or trivet.
4. Place the patties on the trivet or steamer basket,
5. Lock lid into place and set on the MANUAL setting for 2 minutes.
6. When the timer beeps, press "Cancel" and carefully flip the Quick Release valve to let the pressure out.
7. Once all of the pressure releases, the steam will no longer come out of the vent, and you'll be able to open the lid.
8. Remove patties from the pot, and allow to cool down completely.
9. Place patties in a sealed container, and keep refrigerated up to 5 days.

Nutrition Facts

Percent daily values based on the Reference Daily Intake (RDI) for a 2000 calorie diet.

Amount Per Serving

Calories 434.5 | Calories From Fat (75%) 326.68 | Total Fat 38.23g 59% | Saturated Fat 3.8g 19% | Cholesterol 0.77mg <1% | Sodium 47.45mg 2% | Potassium 545.15mg 16% | Total Carbohydrates 16.72g 6% | Fiber 6.71g 27% | Sugar 5g | Protein 12g 24%

Roasted Cabbage Wedges

Ready in Time: 45 minutes | Servings: 6

Ingredients

1 medium head of cabbage cut into wedges

1/2 cup of extra-virgin olive oil

1 tsp red pepper flakes

2 tsp garlic powder

1 tsp kosher salt or to taste

2 Tbsp fresh lemon juice (2 lemons)

Instructions

1. Preheat oven to 420 F.
2. Line a large baking sheet with foil and brush it with olive oil; set aside.
3. Clean cabbage and remove any damaged outer leaves.
4. Cut it in half, then into quarters and wedges.
5. Place the cabbage wedges in a single layer on the prepared baking sheet.
6. Whisk the olive oil, red pepper flakes, garlic powder, salt, and lemon juice in a bowl.
7. Pour the oil mixture evenly over the cabbage wedges.
8. Bake for 15 minutes, and then flip cabbage and bake for further 15 minutes.
9. Remove from the oven and allow to cool down completely.
10. Store the cabbage wedges in large covered airtight containers up to 4 days.

Nutrition Facts

Percent daily values based on the Reference Daily Intake (RDI) for a 2000 calorie diet.

Amount Per Serving

Calories 201.46 | Calories From Fat (80%) 160.57 | Total Fat 18.17g 28% | Saturated Fat 2.54g 13% | Cholesterol 0mg 0% | Sodium 341.58mg 14% | Potassium 274.8mg 8% | Total Carbohydrates 9.7g 3% | Fiber 3.8g 16% | Sugar 4.5g | Protein 2.12g 4%

Row Pistachio Flaxseed Patties

Ready in Time: 15 minutes | Servings: 2

Ingredients

1 cup pistachio finely sliced

1/2 cup ground flaxseed

2 lemon juice from 2 lemons, freshly squeezed

4 cloves garlic minced or mashed

4 Tbsp olive oil

1 Tbsp fresh parsley finely chopped

1 tsp paprika sweet, powder

salt and black pepper to taste

Instructions

1. Add all ingredients in a food processor.
2. Process until well combined.
3. Shape a mixture into two large or four small patties.
4. Store in an airtight container with parchment paper between each patty.
5. Keep in a fridge for up to two weeks.

Nutrition Facts

Percent daily values based on the Reference Daily Intake (RDI) for a 2000 calorie diet.

Amount Per Serving

Calories 606.94 | Calories From Fat (78%) 473.81 | Total Fat 55.1g 85% | Saturated Fat 7.18g 36% | Cholesterol 0mg 0% | Sodium 3.83mg <1% | Potassium 726.13mg 21% | Total Carbohydrates 23.1g 8% | Fiber 6.7g 27% | Sugar 6.28g | Protein 13.11g 26%

Seasoned Spinach Patties

Ready in Time: 25 minutes | Servings: 6

Ingredients

1/2 lb of spinach cooked
1 small onion
1/2 cup of chickpea flour
3/4 cup almond flour
1/3 cup of olive oil
1 tsp garlic powder
1/4 tsp paprika powder
1/4 tsp turmeric powder
Salt and ground pepper to taste

Instructions

1. Boil spinach in salted water for about 5 minutes over medium heat.
2. Remove spinach to a colander, rinse and drain.
3. Place drained spinach along with all remaining ingredients in your high-speed blender or food processor; blend until combined well.
4. Make 6 patties from the mixture and fry in a large frying pan for about 3 minutes per side.
5. Remove patties onto a plate lined with a parchment paper.
6. Keep refrigerated in a sealed container for up to 5 days.

Nutrition Facts

Percent daily values based on the Reference Daily Intake (RDI) for a 2000 calorie diet.

Amount Per Serving

Calories 235.22 | Calories From Fat (49%) 116 | Total Fat 13.19g 20% | Saturated Fat 1.82g 9% | Cholesterol 0mg 0% | Sodium 264mg 11% | Potassium 426.3mg 12% | Total Carbohydrates 22.34g 7% | Fiber 7.65g 31% | Sugar 2g | Protein 9g 18%

Simple Sweet Potato Chips

Ready in Time: 2 hours and 10 minutes | Servings: 4

Ingredients

2 large sweet potatoes
4 Tbsp olive oil
sea salt to taste

Instructions

1. Preheat oven to 250 F.
2. Line a large baking sheet with parchment paper; set aside.
3. Rinse and dry your sweet potatoes thoroughly and slice them very thin; place in a large deep bowl.
4. Sprinkle the sweet potato slices with olive oil and season generously with the salt; toss to combine well.
5. Place in a single layer on a prepared baking sheet.
6. Bake for about 2 hours; flip once at the halfway point.
7. When ready, remove the sweet potatoes from the oven and allow to cool completely.
8. Store the sweet potato chips in an airtight container and keep at a cold and dark place for up to two weeks.

Nutrition Facts

Percent daily values based on the Reference Daily Intake (RDI) for a 2000 calorie diet.

Amount Per Serving

Calories 119.34 | Calories From Fat (78%) 88.34 | Total Fat 13.5g 21% | Saturated Fat 1.86g 9% | Cholesterol 0mg 0% | Sodium 0.27mg <1% | Potassium 0.14mg <1% | Total Carbohydrates 0g 0% | Fiber 0g 0% | Sugar 0g | Protein 0g 0%

Soft Cauliflower and Pecans Spread

Ready in Time: 30 minutes | Servings: 6

Ingredients

1/2 cup of soaked pecans
1 head cauliflower cut into florets
Salt and freshly ground black pepper
3 Tbsp sesame or olive oil
1 onion finely sliced
4 cloves garlic, thinly sliced
1 cup coconut cream
1 sprig thyme chopped
1 tsp tamari sauce

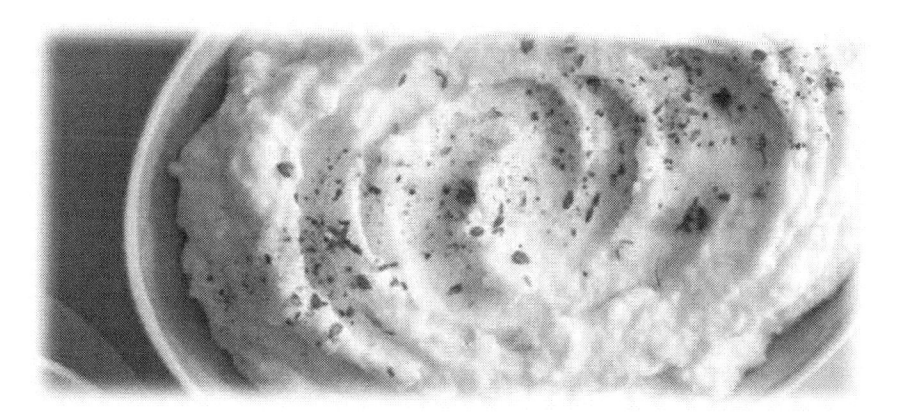

Instructions

1. Soak pecans overnight.
2. Clean cauliflower and divide into florets.
3. Place the cauliflower floret into a large pot and cover with water.
4. Bring to boil and cook for about 6 to 7 minutes over medium-high heat.
5. Remove to a colander and allow it to drain; set aside.
6. In the meantime, heat the oil in a large frying skillet over high heat.
7. Sauté onion and garlic with a pinch of salt for 3 to 4 minutes or until soft.
8. Add cauliflower, pecans, coconut cream, thyme, and tamari sauce; stir for 5 to 6 minutes.
9. Remove from the heat and discard thyme.
10. Using an immersion blender, blend to form a very smooth puree.
11. Season with the salt and pepper to taste.
12. Store into a container and keep refrigerated.

Nutrition Facts

Percent daily values based on the Reference Daily Intake (RDI) for a 2000 calorie diet.

Amount Per Serving

Calories 278,29 | Calories From Fat (84%) 232,44 | Total Fat 27.38g 42% | Saturated Fat 13.7g 69% | Cholesterol 0mg 0% | Sodium 72mg 3% | Potassium 341mg 10% | Total Carbohydrates 8.78g 3% | Fiber 3.12g 12% | Sugar 2.11g | Protein 3.61g 7%

SWEETS/DESSERTS/ENERGYBARS

"Rugged" Coconut Balls

Ready in Time: 15 minutes | Servings: 8

Ingredients

1/3 cup coconut oil melted

1/3 cup coconut butter softened

2 oz coconut, finely shredded, unsweetened

4 Tbsp coconut palm sugar

1/2 cup shredded coconut

Instructions

1. Combine all ingredients in a blender.
2. Blend until soft and well combined.
3. Form small balls from the mixture and roll in shredded coconut.
4. Place on a sheet lined with parchment paper and refrigerate overnight.
5. Keep coconut balls into sealed container in fridge up to one week.

Nutrition Facts

Percent daily values based on the Reference Daily Intake (RDI) for a 2000 calorie diet.

Amount Per Serving

Calories 226.89 | Calories From Fat (84%) 190.39 | Total Fat 21.6g 34% | Saturated Fat 19.84g 99% | Cholesterol 0mg 0% | Sodium 17.19mg <1% | Potassium 45mg 1% | Total Carbohydrates 9g 3% | Fiber 1.16g 5% | Sugar 5.7g | Protein 1g 2%

Almond - Choco Cake

Ready in Time: 45 minutes | Servings: 8

Ingredients

1 1/2 cups of almond flour
1/3 cup almonds finely chopped
1/4 cup of cocoa powder unsweetened
Pinch of salt
1/2 tsp baking soda
2 Tbsp almond milk
1/2 cup Coconut oil melted
2 tsp pure vanilla extract
1/3 cup brown sugar (packed)

Instructions

1. Preheat oven to 350 F.
2. Line 9" cake pan with parchment paper, and grease with a little melted coconut oil; set aside.
3. Stir the almond flour, chopped almonds, cocoa powder, salt, and baking soda in a bowl.
4. In a separate bowl, stir the remaining ingredients.
5. Combine the almond flour mixture with the almond milk mixture and stir well.
6. Place batter in a prepared cake pan.
7. Bake for 30 to 32 minutes.
8. Remove from the oven, allow it to cool completely.
9. Store the cake-slices a freezer, tightly wrapped in a double layer of plastic wrap and a layer of foil. It will keep on this way for up to a month.

Nutrition Facts

Percent daily values based on the Reference Daily Intake (RDI) for a 2000 calorie diet.

Amount Per Serving

Calories 195.61 | Calories From Fat (74%) 145.59 | Total Fat 16.9g 26% | Saturated Fat 12.23g 61% | Cholesterol 0mg 0% | Sodium 118.39mg 5% | Potassium 95.64mg 3% | Total Carbohydrates 11.9g 4% | Fiber 1.52g 6% | Sugar 9.35g | Protein 1.75g 4%

Banana-Almond Cake

Ready in Time: 1 hour | Servings: 8

Ingredients

4 ripe bananas in chunks
3 Tbsš honey or maple syrup
1 tsp pure vanilla extract
1/2 cup almond milk
3/4 cup of self-raising flour
1 tsp cinnamon
1 tsp baking powder
1 pinch of salt
1/3 cup of almonds finely chopped
Almond slices for decoration

Instructions

1. Preheat the oven to 400 F (air mode).
2. Oil a cake mold; set aside.
3. Add bananas into a bowl and mash with the fork.
4. Add honey, vanilla, almond, and stir well.
5. In a separate bowl, stir flour, cinnamon, baking powder, salt, the almonds broken, and mix with a spoon.
6. Combine the flour mixture with the banana mixture, and stir until all ingredients combined well.
7. Transfer the mixture to prepared cake mold and sprinkle with sliced almonds.
8. Bake for 40-45 minutes or until the toothpick inserted comes out clean.
9. Remove from the oven, and allow the cake to cool completely.
10. Cut cake into slices, place in tin foil, or an airtight container, and keep refrigerated up to one week.

Nutrition Facts

Percent daily values based on the Reference Daily Intake (RDI) for a 2000 calorie diet.

Amount Per Serving

Calories 155.94 | Calories From Fat (18%) 27.68 | Total Fat 3.31g 5% | Saturated Fat 0.32g 2% | Cholesterol 0mg 0% | Sodium 98.68mg 4% | Potassium 271mg 8% | Total Carbohydrates 30.61g 10% | Fiber 2.67g 11% | Sugar 14g | Protein 3.6g 7%

Banana-Coconut Ice Cream

Ready in Time: 15 minutes | Servings: 6

Ingredients

1 cup coconut cream
1/2 cup Inverted sugar
2 large frozen bananas (chunks)
3 Tbsp honey extracted
1/4 tsp cinnamon powder

Instructions

1. In a bowl, whip the coconut cream with the inverted sugar.

2. In a separate bowl, beat the banana with honey and cinnamon.

3. Incorporate the coconut whipped cream and banana mixture; stir well.

4. Cover the bowl and let cool in the refrigerator over the night.

5. Stir the mixture 3 to 4 times to avoid crystallization.

6. Keep frozen 1 to 2 months.

Nutrition Facts

Percent daily values based on the Reference Daily Intake (RDI) for a 2000 calorie diet.

Amount Per Serving

Calories 253 | Calories From Fat (46%) 117.23 | Total Fat 14g 22% | Saturated Fat 12.35g 62% | Cholesterol 0mg 0% | Sodium 2.45mg <1% | Potassium 275.25mg 8% | Total Carbohydrates 34.16g 11% | Fiber 1.97g 8% | Sugar 27.19g | Protein 1.91g 4%

Coconut Butter Clouds Cookies

Ready in Time: 25 minutes | Servings: 8

Ingredients

1/2 cup coconut butter softened
1/2 cup peanut butter softened
1/2 cup of granulated sugar
1/2 cup of brown sugar
2 Tbsp chia seeds soaked in 4 tablespoons water
1/2 tsp pure vanilla extract
1/2 tsp baking soda
1/4 tsp salt
1 cup of all-purpose flour

Instructions

1. Preheat oven to 360 F.
2. Add coconut butter, peanut butter, and both sugars in a mixing bowl.
3. Beat with a mixer until soft and sugar combined well.
4. Add soaked chia seeds and vanilla extract; beat.
5. Add baking soda, salt, and flour; beat until all ingredients are combined well.
6. With your hands, shape dough into cookies.
7. Arrange your cookies onto a baking sheet, and bake for about 10 minutes.
8. Remove cookies from the oven and allow to cool completely.
9. Sprinkle with icing sugar and enjoy your cookies.
10. Place cookies in an airtight container and keep refrigerated up to 10 days.

Nutrition Facts

Percent daily values based on the Reference Daily Intake (RDI) for a 2000 calorie diet.

Amount Per Serving

Calories 370.52 | Calories From Fat (50%) 186.69 | Total Fat 21.9g 34% | Saturated Fat 13.5g 68% | Cholesterol 0mg 0% | Sodium 229.6mg 10% | Potassium 140.31mg 4% | Total Carbohydrates 41.1g 14% | Fiber 1.39g 6% | Sugar 27.38g | Protein 5.68g 11%

Chocomint Hazelnut Bars

Ready in Time: 20 minutes | Servings: 8

Ingredients

1/2 cup coconut oil, melted
4 Tbsp cocoa powder
1/4 cup almond butter
3/4 cup brown sugar - (packed)
1 tsp vanilla extract
1 tsp pure peppermint extract
pinch of salt
1 cup shredded coconut
1 cup hazelnuts sliced

Instructions

1. Chop the hazelnuts in a food processor; set aside.

2. Fill the bottom of a double boiler with water and place it on low heat.

3. Put the coconut oil, cacao powder, almond butter, brown sugar, vanilla, peppermint extract, and salt in the top of a double boiler over hot (not boiling) water and constantly stir for 10 minutes.

4. Add hazelnuts and shredded coconut to the melted mixture and stir together.

5. Pour the mixture in a dish lined with parchment and freeze for several hours.

6. Remove from the freezer and cut into bars.

7. Store in airtight container or freezer bag in a freezer.

8. Let the bars at room temperature for 10 to 15 minutes before eating.

Nutrition Facts

Percent daily values based on the Reference Daily Intake (RDI) for a 2000 calorie diet.

Amount Per Serving

Calories 367.25 | Calories From Fat (66%) 243.32 | Total Fat 28.6g 44% | Saturated Fat 14.37g 72% | Cholesterol 0mg 0% | Sodium 38.33mg 2% | Potassium 253.9mg 7% | Total Carbohydrates 28.58g 10% | Fiber 3.56g 14% | Sugar 23.12g | Protein 4.49g 9%

Coco-Cinnamon Balls

Ready in Time: 15 minutes | Servings: 12

Ingredients

1 cup coconut butter softened

1 cup coconut milk canned

1 tsp pure vanilla extract

3/4 tsp cinnamon

1/2 tsp nutmeg

2 Tbsp coconut palm sugar (or granulated sugar)

1 cup coconut shreds

Instructions

1. Combine all ingredients (except the coconut shreds) in a heated bath - bain-marie.

2. Cook and stir until all ingredients are soft and well combined.

3. Remove bowl from heat, place into a bowl, and refrigerate until the mixture firmed up.

4. Form cold coconut mixture into balls, and roll each ball in the shredded coconut.

5. Store into a sealed container, and keep refrigerated up to one week.

Nutrition Facts

Percent daily values based on the Reference Daily Intake (RDI) for a 2000 calorie diet.

Amount Per Serving

Calories 225.6 | Calories From Fat (93%) 209.22 | Total Fat 24.5g 38% | Saturated Fat 21.28g 106% | Cholesterol 0mg 0% | Sodium 3.84mg <1% | Potassium 66.71mg 2% | Total Carbohydrates 3.5g 1% | Fiber 0.71g 3% | Sugar 1.68g | Protein 0.61g 1%

Express Coconut Flax Pudding

Ready in Time: 15 minutes | Servings: 4

Ingredients

1 Tbsp coconut oil softened

1 Tbsp coconut cream

2 cups coconut milk canned

3/4 cup ground flax seed

4 Tbsp coconut palm sugar (or to taste)

Instructions

1. Press SAUTÉ button on your Instant Pot

2. Add coconut oil, coconut cream, coconut milk, and ground flaxseed.

3. Stir about 5 - 10 minutes.

4. Lock lid into place and set on the MANUAL setting for 5 minutes.

5. When the timer beeps, press "Cancel" and carefully flip the Quick Release valve to let the pressure out.

6. Add the palm sugar and stir well.

7. Taste and adjust sugar to taste.

8. Allow pudding to cool down completely.

9. Place the pudding in an airtight container and refrigerate for up to 2 weeks.

Nutrition Facts

Percent daily values based on the Reference Daily Intake (RDI) for a 2000 calorie diet.

Amount Per Serving

Calories 446.5 | Calories From Fat (75%) 334.39 | Total Fat 39.4g 61% | Saturated Fat 25.46g 127% | Cholesterol 0mg 0% | Sodium 23.42mg <1% | Potassium 485.7mg 14% | Total Carbohydrates 21.9g 7% | Fiber 7.94g 32% | Sugar 7.6g | Protein 7.61g 15%

Full-flavored Vanilla Ice Cream

Ready in Time: 15 minutes | Servings: 8

Ingredients

1 1/2 cups canned coconut milk

1 cup coconut whipping cream

1 frozen banana cut into chunks

1 cup vanilla sugar

3 Tbsp apple sauce

2 tsp pure vanilla extract

1 tsp Xanthan gum or agar-agar thickening agent

Instructions

1. Add all ingredients in a food processor; process until all ingredients combined well.

2. Place the ice cream mixture in a freezer-safe container with a lid over.

3. Freeze for at least 4 hours.

4. Remove frozen mixture to a bowl and beat with a mixer to break up the ice crystals.

5. Repeat this process 3 to 4 times.

6. Let the ice cream at room temperature for 15 minutes before serving.

Nutrition Facts

Percent daily values based on the Reference Daily Intake (RDI) for a 2000 calorie diet.

Amount Per Serving

Calories 238.47 | Calories From Fat (68%) 163.29 | Total Fat 19.51g 30% | Saturated Fat 17.26g 86% | Cholesterol 0mg 0% | Sodium 8.24mg <1% | Potassium 268.5mg 8% | Total Carbohydrates 8.8g 3% | Fiber 1.1g 4% | Sugar 4.12g | Protein 2.12g 4%

Irresistible Peanut Cookies

Ready in Time: 25 minutes | Servings: 8

Ingredients

4 Tbsp all-purpose flour
1 tsp baking soda
pinch of salt
1/3 cup granulated sugar
1/3 cup peanut butter softened
3 Tbsp applesauce
1/2 tsp pure vanilla extract

Instructions

1. Preheat oven to 350 F.
2. Combine the flour, baking soda, salt, and sugar in a mixing bowl; stir.
3. Add all remaining ingredients and stir well to form a dough.
4. Roll dough into cookie balls/patties.
5. Arrange your cookies onto greased (with oil or cooking spray) baking sheet.
6. Bake for about 8 to 10 minutes.
7. Let cool for at least 15 minutes before removing from tray.
8. Remove cookies from the tray and let cool completely.
9. Place your peanut butter cookies in an airtight container, and keep refrigerated up to 10 days.

Nutrition Facts

Percent daily values based on the Reference Daily Intake (RDI) for a 2000 calorie diet.

Amount Per Serving

Calories 112.39 | Calories From Fat (42%) 46.73 | Total Fat 5.58g 9% | Saturated Fat 1.15g 6% | Cholesterol 0mg 0% | Sodium 206.8mg 9% | Potassium 82.81mg 2% | Total Carbohydrates 13.82g 5% | Fiber 0.84g 3% | Sugar 9.93g | Protein 3.1g 6%

Murky Almond Cookies

Ready in Time: 25 minutes | Servings: 12

Ingredients

4 Tbsp cocoa powder
2 cups almond flour
1/4 tsp salt
1/2 tsp baking soda
5 Tbsp coconut oil melted
2 Tbsp almond milk
1 1/2 tsp almond extract
1 tsp vanilla extract
4 Tbsp corn syrup or honey

Instructions

1. Preheat oven to 340 F degrees.
2. Grease a large baking sheet; set aside.
3. Combine the cocoa powder, almond flour, salt, and baking soda in a bowl.
4. In a separate bowl, whisk melted coconut oil, almond milk, almond and vanilla extract, and corn syrup or honey.
5. Combine the almond flour mixture with the almond milk mixture and stir until all ingredients incorporate well.
6. Roll tablespoons of the dough into balls, and arrange onto a prepared baking sheet.
7. Bake for 12 to 15 minutes.
8. Remove from the oven and transfer onto a plate lined with a paper towel.
9. Allow cookies to cool down completely and store in an airtight container at room temperature for about four days.

Nutrition Facts

Percent daily values based on the Reference Daily Intake (RDI) for a 2000 calorie diet.

Amount Per Serving

Calories 78.31 | Calories From Fat (68%) 53.17 | Total Fat 5.94g 9% | Saturated Fat 5.48g 27% | Cholesterol 0.2mg <1% | Sodium 39.62mg 2% | Potassium 35.27mg 1% | Total Carbohydrates 6.8g 2% | Fiber 0.61g 2% | Sugar 5.5g | Protein 0.46g <1%

Orange Semolina Halva

Ready in Time: 35 minutes | Servings: 12

Ingredients

6 cups fresh orange juice

Zest from 3 oranges

3 cups brown sugar

1 1/4 cup semolina flour

1 Tbsp almond butter (plain, unsalted)

4 Tbsp ground almond

1/4 tsp cinnamon

Instructions

1. Heat the orange juice, orange zest with brown sugar in a pot.

2. Stir over medium heat until sugar is dissolved.

3. Add the semolina flour and cook over low heat for 15 minutes; stir occasionally.

4. Add almond butter, ground almonds, and cinnamon, and stir well.

5. Cook, frequently stirring, for further 5 minutes.

6. Transfer the halva mixture into a mold, let it cool and refrigerate for at least 4 hours.

7. Keep refrigerated in a sealed container for one week.

Nutrition Facts

Percent daily values based on the Reference Daily Intake (RDI) for a 2000 calorie diet.

Amount Per Serving

Calories 352.85 | Calories From Fat (6%) 22.34 | Total Fat 2.67g 4% | Saturated Fat 0.23g 1% | Cholesterol 0mg 0% | Sodium 17mg <1% | Potassium 384.18mg 11% | Total Carbohydrates 80.42g 27% | Fiber 1.41g 6% | Sugar 63.8g | Protein 4.03g 8%

Seasoned Cinnamon Mango Popsicles

Ready in Time: 15 minutes | Servings: 6

Ingredients

1 1/2 cups of mango pulp

1 mango cut in cubes

1 cup brown sugar (packed)

2 Tbsp lemon juice freshly squeezed

1 tsp cinnamon

1 pinch of salt

Instructions

1. Add all ingredients into your blender.
2. Blend until brown sugar dissolved.
3. Pour the mango mixture evenly in popsicle molds or cups.
4. Insert sticks into each mold.
5. Place molds in a freezer, and freeze for at least 5 to6 hours.
6. Before serving, un-mold easy your popsicles placing molds under lukewarm water.

Nutrition Facts

Percent daily values based on the Reference Daily Intake (RDI) for a 2000 calorie diet.

Amount Per Serving

Calories 166.47 | Calories From Fat (1%) 1.47 | Total Fat 0.18g <1% | Saturated Fat 0.04g <1% | Cholesterol 0mg 0% | Sodium 59.22mg 2% | Potassium 125.5mg 4% | Total Carbohydrates 42.9g 14% | Fiber 1g 4% | Sugar 41.39g | Protein 0.42g <1%

Strawberry Molasses Ice Cream

Ready in Time: 20 minutes | Servings: 8

Ingredients

1 lb strawberries

3/4 cup coconut palm sugar (or granulated sugar)

1 cup coconut cream

1 Tbsp molasses

1 tsp balsamic vinegar

1/2 tsp agar-agar

1/2 tsp pure strawberry extract

Instructions

1. Add strawberries, date sugar, and the balsamic vinegar in a blender; blend until completely combined.

2. Place the mixture in the refrigerator for one hour.

3. In a mixing bowl, beat the coconut cream with an electric mixer to make a thick mixture.

4. Add molasses, balsamic vinegar, agar-agar, and beat for further one minute or until combined well.

5. Add the strawberry mixture and beat again for 2 minutes.

6. Pour ice cream mix into an ice cream maker, turn on the machine, and churn according to manufacturer's directions.

7. Keep frozen in a freezer-safe container (with plastic film and lid over).

Nutrition Facts

Percent daily values based on the Reference Daily Intake (RDI) for a 2000 calorie diet.

Amount Per Serving

Calories 184.23 | Calories From Fat (48%) 88.3 | Total Fat 10.58g 16% | Saturated Fat 9.23g 46% | Cholesterol 0mg 0% | Sodium 2.87mg <1% | Potassium 221.8mg 6% | Total Carbohydrates 23g 8% | Fiber 1.9g 7% | Sugar 15g | Protein 1.47g 3%

Strawberry-Mint Sorbet

Ready in Time: 15 minutes | Servings: 6

Ingredients

1 cup of granulated sugar
1 cup of orange juice
1 lb frozen strawberries
1 tsp pure peppermint extract

Instructions

1. Add sugar and orange juice in a saucepan.
2. Stir over high heat and boil for 5 minutes or until sugar dissolves.
3. Remove from the heat and let it cool down.
4. Add strawberries into a blender, and blend until smooth.
5. Pour syrup into strawberries, add peppermint extract and stir until all ingredients combined well.
6. Transfer mixture to a storage container, cover tightly, and freeze until ready to serve.

Nutrition Facts

Percent daily values based on the Reference Daily Intake (RDI) for a 2000 calorie diet.

Amount Per Serving

Calories 167.86 | Calories From Fat (1%) 1.15 | Total Fat 0.14g <1% | Saturated Fat 0.01g <1% | Cholesterol 0mg 0% | Sodium 2.12mg <1% | Potassium 167.7mg 5% | Total Carbohydrates 43g 14% | Fiber 1.64g 7% | Sugar 39g | Protein 0.52g 1%

Vegan Choco - Hazelnut Spread

Ready in Time: 15 minutes | Servings: 6

Ingredients

1 cup hazelnuts soaked
4 Tbsp dry cacao powder
4 Tbsp Maple syrup
1 tsp pure vanilla extract
1/4 tsp Kosher salt
4 Tbsp almond milk

Instructions

1. Soak hazelnuts with water overnight.
2. Add soaked hazelnuts along with all remaining ingredients in a food processor.
3. Process for about 10 minutes or until a cream get the desired consistency.
4. Keep the spread in a sealed container refrigerated up to 2 weeks.

Nutrition Facts

Percent daily values based on the Reference Daily Intake (RDI) for a 2000 calorie diet.

Amount Per Serving

Calories 289 | Calories From Fat (70%) 201.61 | Total Fat 24g 37% | Saturated Fat 2g 10% | Cholesterol 0mg 0% | Sodium 80.75mg 3% | Potassium 369.56mg 11% | Total Carbohydrates 17.6g 6% | Fiber 4.75g 19% | Sugar 10g | Protein 6,39g 13%

Vegan Exotic Chocolate Mousse

Ready in Time: 10 minutes | Servings: 5

Instructions

2 frozen bananas chunks
2 avocados
1/3 cup of dates
4 Tbsp cocoa powder
1/2 cup of fresh orange juice
zest, from 1 orange

Instructions

1. Add bananas, avocado, and dates in a food processor.
2. Process for about 2 to 3 minutes until combined well.
3. Add cocoa powder, orange juice, and orange zest; process for further one minute.
4. Place cream in a glass jar or container and keep refrigerated up to one week.

Nutrition Facts

Percent daily values based on the Reference Daily Intake (RDI) for a 2000 calorie diet.

Amount Per Serving

Calories 213.56 | Calories From Fat (45%) 96.53 | Total Fat 11.51g 18% | Saturated Fat 1.88g 9% | Cholesterol 0mg 0% | Sodium 7.5mg <1% | Potassium 716.42mg 20% | Total Carbohydrates 31.13g 10% | Fiber 8.53g 34% | Sugar 15.65g | Protein 3.21g 6%

Vegan Lemon Pudding

Ready in Time: 20 minutes | Servings: 3

Ingredients

2 cups almond milk
3 Tbsp of cornflour
2 Tbsp of all-purpose flour
1 cup of sugar granulated
1/4 cup almond butter (plain, unsalted)
1 tsp lemon zest
1/3 cup fresh lemon juice

Instructions

1. Add the almond milk with cornflour, flour, and sugar in a saucepan.

2. Cook, frequently stirring, until sugar dissolved, and all ingredients combine well (for about 5 to 7 minutes over medium heat).

3. Add the almond butter, lemon zest, and lemon juice.

4. Cook, frequently stirring, for further 5 to 6 minutes.

5. Remove the lemon pudding from the heat and allow it to cool completely.

6. Pour into the sealed container and keep refrigerated up to one week.

Nutrition Facts

Percent daily values based on the Reference Daily Intake (RDI) for a 2000 calorie diet.

Amount Per Serving

Calories 178.8 | Calories From Fat (52%) 93.14 | Total Fat 11.5g 18% | Saturated Fat 0.92g 5% | Cholesterol 0mg 0% | Sodium 2.21mg <1% | Potassium 208.57mg 6% | Total Carbohydrates 18.58g 6% | Fiber 2.86g 11% | Sugar 1.63g | Protein 5.7g 12%

Vitamin Blast Tropical Sherbet

Preparation Time: 15 minutes | Servings: 10

Ingredients

4 cups mangos pitted and cut into 1/2-inch dice

1 papaya cut into 1/2-inch dice

1/4 cup granulated sugar or honey (optional)

1 cup pineapple juice canned

1/4 cup coconut milk

2 Tbsp coconut cream

1 fresh lime juice

Instructions

1. Add all ingredients into your food processor; process until all ingredients smooth and combine well.
2. Transfer the mixture to a bowl, cover, and refrigerate for about 2 hours.
3. Remove the sherbet mixture from the fridge, stir well, and pour in a freezer-safe container (with plastic film and lid over).
4. Keep frozen.
5. Let the sherbet at room temperature for 15 minutes before serving.

Nutrition Facts

Percent daily values based on the Reference Daily Intake (RDI) for a 2000 calorie diet.

Amount Per Serving

Calories 104.15 | Calories From Fat (16%) 16.96 | Total Fat 2g 3% | Saturated Fat 1.5g 8% | Cholesterol 0mg 0% | Sodium 3mg <1% | Potassium 214.95mg 6% | Total Carbohydrates 22.54g 8% | Fiber 1.68g 7% | Sugar 17.2g | Protein 1.2g 2%

Walnut Vanilla Popsicles

Ready in Time: 15 minutes | Servings: 8

Ingredients

1 1/2 cup finely sliced walnuts
4 cups of almond milk
4 Tbsp brown sugar (packed)
1 scoop protein powder (pea or soy)
2 tsp pure vanilla extract

Instructions

1. Add all ingredients in your high-speed blender and blend until smooth and combined well.

2. Pour the mixture in popsicle molds and insert the wooden stick into the middle of each mold.

3. Freeze until your ice popsicles are completely frozen.

4. Serve and enjoy!

Nutrition Facts

Percent daily values based on the Reference Daily Intake (RDI) for a 2000 calorie diet.

Amount Per Serving

Calories 212.59 | Calories From Fat (69%) 147.22 | Total Fat 16.7g 26% | Saturated Fat 1.4g 7% | Cholesterol 0.05mg <1% | Sodium 142.8mg 6% | Potassium 108.2mg 3% | Total Carbohydrates 11.47g 4% | Fiber 1.47g 6% | Sugar 7.46g | Protein 4.37g 9%

About the Author

Joseph P. Turner has spent his life learning what makes a healthy lifestyle and how to train our bodies to achieve maximum potential. What makes his journey more incredible is he has learned how to do all this while being vegan. He believes that we can each achieve optimum health without compromising our core values and maintaining a healthy lifestyle without the chemicals and preservatives that go into most good. His healthy living approach is both simple and easy to maintain.

His first book is the Meatless Power Cookbook for Vegan Athletes. It focuses on his own personal recipes as well as several he has discovered over the years to trim the fat, lose weight, and feel good in the process.

Joseph is a certified fitness trainer and nutritionist. When he is not in the gym Joseph can be found hard at work in the kitchen whipping up his favorite meals or creating new, delicious dishes. Writing may be his latest endeavor, but cooking has always been his true passion.

One Last Thing...

DID YOU ENJOY THE BOOK?

IF SO, THEN LET ME KNOW BY LEAVING A REVIEW ON AMAZON! Reviews are the lifeblood of independent authors. I would appreciate even a few words and rating if that's all you have time for

IF YOU DID NOT LIKE THIS BOOK, THEN PLEASE TELL ME! Email me at perfectecruz@gmail.com and let me know what you didn't like! Perhaps I can change it. In today's world, a book doesn't have to be stagnant; it can improve with time and feedback from readers like you. You can impact this book, and I welcome your feedback. Help make this book better for everyone!

Made in the USA
San Bernardino, CA
29 May 2020